THE LAST YEARS
OF POLISH JEWRY

The Last Years of Polish Jewry

by Yankev Leshchinsky

Volume 2: The Permanent Pogrom, 1935–37

Translated by Robert Brym and Eli Jany
Edited and with an Introduction by Robert Brym

https://www.openbookpublishers.com/
©2024 Translation Robert Brym and Eli Jany. ©2024 Introduction and notes Robert Brym

This work is licensed under an Attribution-NonCommercial 4.0 International (CC BY-NC 4.0). This license allows you to share, copy, distribute and transmit the text; to adapt the text for non-commercial purposes of the text providing attribution is made to the authors (but not in any way that suggests that they endorse you or your use of the work).

Attribution should include the following information:

Yankev Leshchinsky, *The Last Years of Polish Jewry. Volume 2: The Permanent Pogrom, 1935–37*. Edited by Robert Brym; translated by Robert Brym and Eli Jany. Cambridge, UK: Open Book Publishers, 2024, https://doi.org/10.11647/OBP.0342

Further details about the CC BY-NC license are available at
http://creativecommons.org/licenses/by-nc/4.0/

All external links were active at the time of publication unless otherwise stated and have been archived via the Internet Archive Wayback Machine at https://archive.org/web

Digital material and resources associated with this volume are available at
https://doi.org/10.11647/OBP.0342#resources

Copyright and permissions for the reuse of many of the images included in this publication differ from the above. This information is provided in the captions and in the list of illustrations. Every effort has been made to identify and contact copyright holders and any omission or error will be corrected if notification is made to the publisher.

ISBN Paperback: 978-1-80064-997-2
ISBN Hardback: 978-1-80064-998-9
ISBN Digital (PDF): 978-1-80064-999-6
ISBN Digital ebook (EPUB): 978-1-80511-000-2
ISBN Digital ebook (HTML): 978-1-80511-003-3
DOI: 10.11647/OBP.0342

Cover photo: Selling old clothes in a Jewish market in interwar Warsaw (undated), Warsaw, Poland. ©Yad Vashem Photo Archive, Jerusalem, https://photos.yadvashem.org/photo-details.html?language=en&item_id=24526&ind=123

Cover design: Jeevanjot Kaur Nagpal

Contents

List of figures	vii
Introduction	1
Robert Brym	
About the translation and the translators	11

Part 1: Pogroms

1. The pogroms in Poland, 1935–37	15
2. Pogrom gunpowder	75
3. The Minsk-Mazovyetsk pogrom	83
4. The Pshitik pogrom	89

Part 2: Official antisemitism

5. Government antisemitism	109
6. The first ghetto benches in the universities	115
7. Ghetto benches	121

Part 3: Jewish responses

8. Jewish self-defence	127
9. Protests against pogroms	133
10. Old-fashioned methods in new times	147
11. Suicides	153
12. Is emigration a solution?	159
13. Jews flee Poland	165

References	173
Index	175

List of figures

Fig. 1 The Mishlenitse pogromists on the way to trial, May 1937. Polish National Digital Archives, public domain, https://www.szukajwarchiwach.gov.pl/en/wyszukiwarka   2

Fig. 2 Poland, August 1939. The locations of twelve anti-Jewish riots that took place between 1935 and 1937 and are referred to as pogroms in the literature. Modified from Wikimedia, CC BY-SA, https://en.wikipedia.org/wiki/File:Map_of_Poland_August_1939.png   3

Fig. 3 Mourners follow a horse-drawn hearse carrying Khaya Minkovski, murdered in the 1936 pogrom in Pshitik. ©Archives of the YIVO Institute for Jewish Research, New York, http://polishjews.yivoarchives.org/archive/index.php?p=digitallibrary/digitalcontent&id=4526   7

Fig. 4 Members of the Bund marching on 1 May 1936, Warsaw. ©Yad Vashem Photo Archive, Jerusalem, archive item 1605_626, https://photos.yadvashem.org/photo-details.html?language=en&item_id=10143&ind=3   33

Fig. 5 People examining a house that was burned down in the 1936 Minsk-Mazovyetsk pogrom. ©Archives of the YIVO Institute for Jewish Research, New York, http://polishjews.yivoarchives.org/archive/index.php?p=digitallibrary/digitalcontent&id=2804   54

Fig. 6 Victims of the Minsk-Mazovyetsk pogrom (June 1936). Wikimedia, public domain, https://commons.wikimedia.org/wiki/File:Ofiary_pogromu_w_Mi%C5%84sku_Mazowieckim_czerwiec_1936.jpg   85

Fig. 7   Demonstration of Endek students at Lvov Polytechnic.   117
        The banner reads: "A Day without Jews: We will
        create an official ghetto." Wikimedia, public
        domain, https://commons.wikimedia.org/wiki/
        File:%C5%BB%C4%85damy_urz%C4%99dowego_getta_
        Ob%C3%B3z_Narodowo-Radykalny_Politechnika_
        Lwowska.jpg

Fig. 8   First pages of the "List of Lectures and Exercises" for   118
        medical school student Marek Szapiro, University of
        Warsaw. The stamp above the photo reads, "SEATING in
        benches with an odd number." Wikimedia, public domain,
        https://commons.wikimedia.org/wiki/File:Index_
        of_Jewish_student_in_Poland_with_Ghetto_benche_
        seal_1934.PNG

Introduction

Robert Brym

On the night of 22 June 1936, about seventy right-wing nationalists entered Mishlenitse (Myślenice), a small town south of Krakow, Poland. They cut the town's telephone cables, commandeered rifles from the local police station, and then turned to their main task: attacking Jewish-owned crockery, grocery, leather goods, and haberdashery shops. They broke windows, destroyed merchandise, and set fires, including one at the local synagogue. Interpersonal violence was not their main goal; they killed no one and assaulted four Jews. Rather, the attackers were seeking to put into practice ideas expressed in a document issued by the Krakow branch of the *Narodowa Demokracja* party. It urged a "fight against Jewish capitalism... [and] for returning to the Polish nation one million trade, craft and industrial workshops, which constitute today the foundation of Jewish power, capable of providing work and bread to all Poles who do not have them today."[1] Twenty months later, in the only verdict pertaining to the Mishlenitse ethnic riot, its leader was found guilty on the sole charge of seizing arms from the police station. He was sentenced to a prison term of three-and-a-half-years, later commuted to one year (Fig. 1).

In the 1930s, Poles referred to incidents like the one in Mishlenitse as "excesses." In contrast, Jews call such events "pogroms." This volume, which collects Yankev Leshchinsky's writings on various aspects of popular and official antisemitism in Poland from 1935 to 1937, focuses on anti-Jewish pogroms and Jewish responses to them.[2]

---

1. According to Leshchinsky, there were actually 250,000 Jewish shops and market stalls and 200,000 Jewish workshops..
2. Originally published in Yiddish as *Erev khurbn: Fun yidishn lebn in poyln, 1935–37*

Fig. 1 The Mishlenitse pogromists on the way to trial, May 1937. Polish National Digital Archives, public domain, https://www.szukajwarchiwach.gov.pl/en/wyszukiwarka

The noun "pogrom" derives from the Russian verb *pogromit'* (погромить), "to destroy" or "to massacre." Recently surveying the history of anti-Jewish pogroms in Eastern Europe from 1881 to 1946, Eugene M. Avrutin and Elissa Bemporad wrote:

> [T]he term "pogrom" characterizes mob attacks or deadly ethnic riots that were usually, but not always, carried out in urban settings....[P]ogrom refers to a constellation of violent events, ranging from spontaneous ethnic riots (resulting in bodily injury, looting or destruction of property, and death) to genocidal violence (the deliberate killing of an a entire group of people).[3]

This definition applies reasonably well to as many as twelve interwar anti-Jewish riots in Poland that are mentioned in the literature. Apart from the events at Mishlenitse, they include pogroms that took place between June 1935 and August 1937 in Grodno, Adzhival (Odrzywoł), Pshitik (Przytyk), Minsk-Mazovyetsk (Mińsk Mazowiecki), Brisk (Brzesc),

---

[*On the Eve of Destruction: On Jewish Life in Poland, 1935–37*] (Buenos Aires: Tsentralfarband fun poylishe yidn in argentina, 1951).

3 Eugene M. Avrutin and Elissa Bemporad, "Pogroms: An Introduction," in *Pogroms: A Documentary History*, ed. by Eugene M. Avrutin and Elissa Bemporad (New York: Oxford University Press, 2021), p. 4.

Dzhedzhgov (Dzierzgowo), Tshenstokhov (Częstochowa), Kelts (Kielce), Warsaw, Vilna (Wilno; Vilnius), and Lomzhe (Łomża) (see Fig. 2). Such pogroms, concentrated in towns and cities running along a diagonal from southwestern to northeastern Poland, resulted in "dozens of casualties" according to Anna Cichopek-Gajraj and Glenn Dynner. In contrast—and testifying to the question of what constitutes a pogrom as much as the difficulty of discovering precise numbers—Antony Polonsky writes that fourteen Jews were killed and "as many as 2,000" injured.[4]

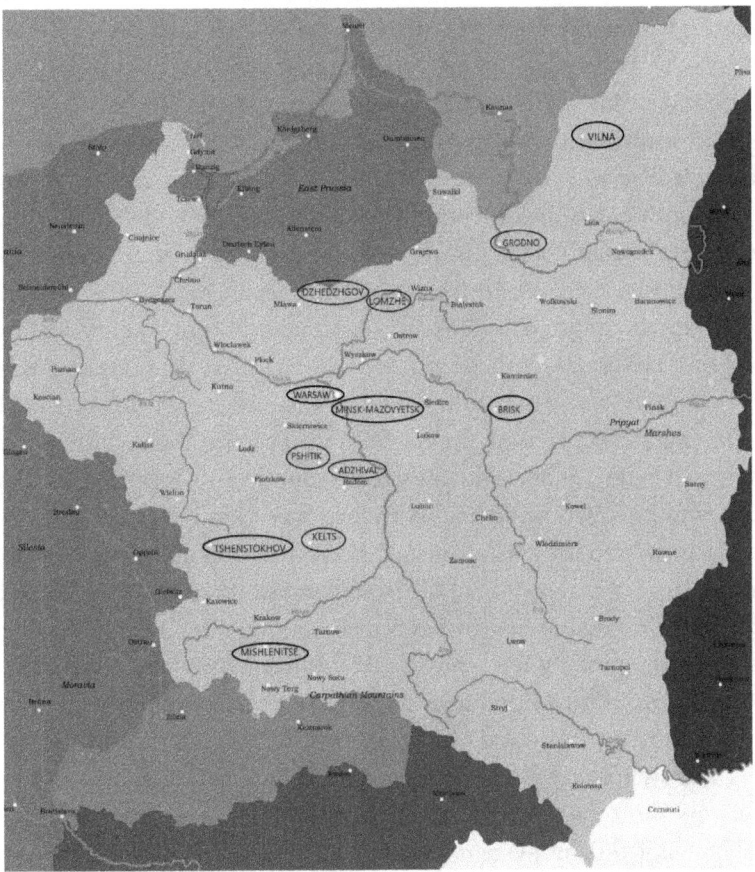

Fig. 2 Poland, August 1939. The locations of twelve anti-Jewish riots that took place between 1935 and 1937 and are referred to as pogroms in the literature. Modified from Wikimedia, CC BY-SA, https://en.wikipedia.org/wiki/File:Map_of_Poland_August_1939.png

---

4   Anna Cichopek-Gajraj and Glenn Dynner, "Pogroms in Modern Poland, 1918–1946," in *Pogroms: A Documentary History*, p. 193; Antony Polonsky, *The Jews of Poland and Russia: A Short History* (Oxford: The Littman Library of Jewish Civilization, 2013), p. 227.

It is evident from the long first essay in this collection that Leshchinsky would have considered these counts of the murdered and injured too low—and Avrutin and Bemporad's definition of "pogrom" too narrow. For one thing, the counts apparently do not take into account people who were seriously injured during a pogrom but died from their injuries long after the rioting ended. Leshchinsky mentions eight known cases: Borekh Zilberberg, one Lutenberg, and Khaim Perlis, who died between two weeks and four months after the Brisk pogrom; Gedalye, Feyge, and Yudl Tishler, who succumbed to their injuries up to six months after the Pshitik pogrom; Khaim Shimenovski, who passed away a year after the Minsk-Mazovyetsk pogrom; and Leyb Shapiro, who died eighteen months after injuries he sustained in the Grodno pogrom.

More importantly, not just in an arithmetic but in a sociological sense, most acts of violence that caused deaths and injuries are not included in conventional tallies of pogrom-related deaths and injuries. From the incidents that historians of interwar Poland commonly identify as pogroms, one is likely to learn that they each involved a few score to perhaps a thousand attackers. Historians do not qualify incidents involving fewer assailants as pogroms. Thus, they do not recognize as a pogrom ten young men attacking Jews strolling or sitting on benches in Warsaw's Saxon Garden, chasing and beating them with wooden sticks, throwing them into the park's pond, and toppling carriages with small Jewish children in them, even though in 1937 similar attacks persisted for weeks on end and resulted in many injuries, some serious. And when just one Pole from a peasant family noticed a sixty-two-year-old Jew passing by his house, ran outside, unprovoked, with an axe, split open the Jew's head, and left him dying in a pool of blood, it is certainly not counted as a pogrom in the conventional definition of the term. Yet thousands of Poles, unprovoked, physically attacked Jews with whom they were unacquainted between 1935 and 1937.

If, on the other hand, one surveys and adds up the carnage, as Leshchinsky did by systematically poring over contemporary Jewish press reports, a picture emerges not of twelve discrete events, each characterized by short time spans of a day or two and participants typically numbering in the scores or hundreds, but of *a single sustained collective event stretching over nearly three years and involving many discrete bursts of property destruction and interpersonal violence, varying widely in duration, intensity, and level of participation*. Specifically, the nationwide collective event targeted Jews in more than 150 Polish towns for beatings, stabbings, bombings, looting, acts of arson, and the vandalization of business and residential property. It was supported above all by the *Narodowa Demokracja* party (*Endecja* for short), which mobilized activists from all Polish social classes. Understanding how deeply entrenched antisemitism was in Poland, the Endeks, as party members were commonly known, intensified their antisemitism partly as a means of outbidding other parties for popular support.[5]

Leshchinsky calls this sociological phenomenon a "permanent pogrom."[6] He recognizes that the number of murdered Jews in the Polish pogroms of 1935–37 was small compared to the more than 100,000 killed in Ukrainian pogroms during the Russian civil war (1918–21).[7] However, Leshchinsky's list of violent anti-Jewish actions allows him to make the credible claim that the permanent pogrom in Poland killed

---

5   In recent decades, historians have sought to demonstrate that antisemitism in interwar Poland was not as widespread as previously believed. See Natalia Aleksiun, *Conscious History: Polish Jewish Historians before the Holocaust* (London: Littman Library of Jewish Civilization, 2021); Gershon Bacon, "Cautious Use of the Term 'Antisemitism'—for Lack of an Alternative: Interwar Poland as a Test Case," in *Antisemitism and the Politics of History*, ed. by Scott Ury and Guy Miron (Waltham MA: Brandeis University Press, 2024 [2020]); Ezra Mendelsohn, 'Interwar Poland: Good for the Jews or Bad for the Jews?," in *The Jews in Poland*, ed. by Chimen Abramsky, Maciej Jachimczyk, and Antony Polonsky (Oxford: Blackwell 1986), pp. 130–39; Jerzy Tomaszewski, "Some Methodological Problems of the Study of Jewish History in Poland between the Two World Wars," in *From Shtetl to Socialism: Studies from Polin*, ed. by Antony Polonsky (Oxford: Littman Library of Jewish Civilization, 1993), pp. 251–63. What remains uncontested is that interwar Poland was among Europe's most antisemitic countries if not its most antisemitic. Nationally representative polls on the subject were of course unknown in Poland until the last few decades. However, history resounds in the consistent modern-day finding that, within sampling error, Poland ranks highest among European countries on antisemitism. To my knowledge, the latest survey on the subject as of this writing was conducted in late 2022. It found that 35% of Polish adults were antisemitic in the sense that they agreed with six or more of eleven negative statements about Jews. At the low end among European countries, Netherland's score was 6%. See Anti-Defamation League, "Poland," 2023, https://global100.adl.org/country/poland/2023.

6   In 1935, Leshchinsky still expressed ambivalence about referring to smaller attacks as part of a countrywide permanent pogrom. His ambivalence disappears in this volume's undated lead essay, which was completed in 1937, although even there he claims that only in Grodno, Pshitik, and Minsk-Mazovyetsk did "real" pogroms occur.

7   Jeffrey Veidlinger, "Anti-Jewish violence in the Russian civil war," in *Pogroms: A Documentary History*, p. 133.

"hundreds" and wounded "as many as 10,000" Jews during the period under consideration (pp. 23, 61, below). He also believed that his numbers are underestimates:

> [T]he material we will use in our work... consists only of newspaper articles that have gone through the highly stringent Polish censor, so the articles are like official acknowledgements. In the editorial archives of all Jewish newspapers there are mountains of material that could not be made public due to censorship....There can be no doubt they were not allowed to be made public because they reflect actual life too clearly. However, we have not used these archival materials (p. 23, below).

In terms of the permanent pogrom's effects, Leshchinsky writes: "It paralyzes the Jewish masses, disorganizes Jewish society, wildly tears livelihoods from Jewish hands, shifting the full attention of the Jewish individual and the Jewish community to fleeing, emigrating, saving oneself; weakening in this way the courage to struggle for the jobs that have been saved." Nonetheless, "[t]he dry numbers derived from the list of the wounded in cities where there were attacks...do not convey even in the palest form and by the weakest measure the truly tragic situation that is signified by the words 'permanent pogrom'" (pp. 57 58, below). The chief emotional consequence of the permanent pogrom was the normalization of fear. Knowing they could be attacked at any time and in any place, most of Poland's 3.1 million Jews walked with cowed heads and tensed shoulders, always ready to bolt in response to the slightest stir.

Yet many refused to bolt. In Warsaw, Lodz, Bialystok, and elsewhere, organized groups of Jewish workers defended Jews from attack, went on the offensive, and occasionally took pre-emptive action. Often, "[a]s soon as a commotion breaks out in the street...youth, workers, porters, and athletes run toward the commotion to defend their battered brothers, to teach the hooligans a lesson and to take revenge on the pogromists".[8]

In 1936, the trial took place of forty-three Poles and fourteen Jews accused of violent crimes during the Pshitik pogrom. Thirty-nine Poles, including the murderers of Khaye and Yosef Minkovski, a Jewish couple,

---

8   Leshchinsky, *Erev khurbn...*, p. 106. The authorities often cited Jewish resistance as evidence that Jews caused the pogrom. See, for example, Adam Penkalla, "The Przytyk Incidents of 9 March 1936 from Archival Documents," *Polin* (5: 2008), 337–40.

were sentenced to light prison terms ranging from one-half to one year. The Jews' entirely credible claim that they were acting in self-defence was rejected by the court. Ten Jews were sentenced to six months in prison and one received a sentence of eight years. Poland's Jewish community erupted in fury. Jewish workers' parties, supported by the Polish Socialist Party, organized a highly effective nationwide strike of Jews. According to Leshchinsky, "[a] quarter of a million Jewish shops and market stalls and 200,000 Jewish workshops closed in unison across all of Poland" (p. 136, below).

Fig. 3 Mourners follow a horse-drawn hearse carrying Khaya Minkovski, murdered in the 1936 pogrom in Pshitik. ©Archives of the YIVO Institute for Jewish Research, New York, http://polishjews.yivoarchives.org/archive/index.php?p=digitallibrary/digitalcontent&id=4526.

The permanent pogrom did not spare universities and high schools, where armed attacks on Jewish students were widespread. In 1935, Jews had begun to be assigned segregated seating at Lvov (Lwów) Polytechnic.[9] Jewish students took to standing in protest during their

---

9   A pamphlet distributed in all Warsaw high schools in 1937 exhorted students, "[D]o not hesitate to be brutal....The words progress, science and democracy may sound very well but behind them is concealed the disgusting Jewish spirit. Remember, if you have a Jew or a Communist in a lonely spot, hit him with an iron bar in his teeth. Do not be afraid and do not feel sorry for him." Quoted in H. Rabinowicz, "The Battle of the Ghetto Benches," *The Jewish Quarterly Review* (55, 2: 1964), 154.

classes. By 1937 the spread of so-called ghetto benches caused Polish Jewry to protest *en masse*.[10] On 19 October, a six-hour closure of all Jewish schools, shops, workshops, factories, banks, cafes, and restaurants in Warsaw took place. It was followed by a "Week for Jewish Students" during which Jews boycotted places of entertainment and refrained from all non-essential expenditures.

Such efforts notwithstanding, Jewish resistance was on the whole piecemeal and ineffective. Leshchinsky notes that some religious Jews prayed and fasted in the hope that God would answer their entreaties. Liberal Jews appealed to the government for more repressive measures against antisemitic rioters. However, for all practical purposes, the government's response was similar to that of the Almighty. The permanent pogrom dragged on. The police continued to arrest many fewer Poles for attacking Jews than they arrested Jews for defending themselves. For their part, the disparate Jewish parties and ideological currents were unable and unwilling to forge a united and steadfast opposition front.

Leshchinsky recognized that the fundamental cause of Poland's permanent pogrom was "economic." Specifically, the industrialization of Poland was incompatible with the ethnic composition of the country's class structure.

Industrialization requires what sociologists call "structural mobility." Agricultural jobs must be turned into jobs for artisans, merchants, industrialists, professionals, and industrial and white-collar workers. However, in Poland, non-Jewish peasants comprised 60% of the Polish labour force according to the 1931 census. Jews, on the other hand, were considerably overrepresented as professionals, greatly overrepresented as artisans, and vastly overrepresented as merchants—precisely the types of jobs Poles sought in increasing number as their undeveloped agricultural system failed to sustain them.[11] Pressured by the forces of capitalist development, the country's extraordinarily high level of ethnic

---

10 Józef Piłatowicz, "Anti-Semitic Resentments at the Universities in the Second Polish Republic on the Example of Lviv (1918–1939 AD)," *Cogent Arts and Humanities* (7, 1: 2020), https://doi.org/10.1080/23311983.2020.1801369

11 Early in Poland's industrialization, Jews had also been overrepresented as industrial workers, largely because of their employment in the Jewish-owned textile factories of Lodz and Bialystok. However, their representation among industrial workers in large factories declined in the 1930s.

stratification increased the likelihood that Poles would seek to remove Jews from various positions in the ethnic stratification system, as the Endek document quoted in this Introduction's first paragraph urged. As the depression deepened, the likelihood increased.

If these structural circumstances set the stage for interethnic violence, largely political circumstances affected the timing, scope, and severity of violence during the permanent pogrom: the growing influence of Nazi Germany on Polish society, chillingly pictured in Fig. 1, above; the increasing hostility of Poland's Catholic Church toward Jews; and the death of Joseph Pilsudki {Józef Piłsudski}, Poland's former Prime Minister, on 12 May 1935.[12]

Pilsudski remained a dominant political figure even after he left office in 1928, balancing authoritarian-centrist and totalitarian-nationalist elements in the ruling *Sanacja* ("healing") party and thereby keeping a lid on interethnic conflict and its violent expression. After his passing, *Sanacja* split into warring factions. Members of its totalitarian-nationalist wing believed that by relaxing sanctions against antisemitic violence the government could increase its appeal to young totalitarian-nationalists and thus limit the growth of parties to its right, including but not restricted to *Endecja*. Their words and actions helped to unleash the permanent pogrom.

In 1937, after nearly three years of bloodshed and destruction, another change in political conditions began to rein in the permanent pogrom. Even before the 1938 Nazi *Anschluss* of Austria, the attention of Polish politicians was deflected from internal ethnic conflict and drawn toward foreign policy and national security issues. Moreover, the Polish government came to view anti-Jewish violence as ineffective if not counterproductive. The opinion grew that replacing Jewish merchants and artisans with Poles would not rid the country of Jews and could not in any case take place on a sufficiently large scale to solve the structural mobility problem since Jews formed just 10% of the country's population. Instead, the government decided that the mass emigration of Jews was required.

To that end, the government now established close contact with Zionist organizations to facilitate the removal of Jews from Polish society.

---

12 The following account is based largely on Polonsky, *The Jews in Poland*..., pp. 225–35 and Emanuel Melzer, *No Way Out: The Politics of Polish Jewry, 1935–1939* (Cincinnati OH: Hebrew Union College Press, 1997), pp. 15–38.

It lobbied the League of Nations in support of Jewish emigration to Palestine, Madagascar, or anywhere else. Little came of this effort. Britain was reluctant to permit the mass migration of Jews to Palestine for fear of further angering its Arab majority. The depression and the spread of fascism ensured that no country was much interested in immigrants, let alone Jewish immigrants. In 1937, only about 9,000 Jews—less than 0.3% of Poland's Jewish community—managed to leave the country.

And so it transpired that Poland's Jews were trapped in a fate immeasurably worse than the permanent pogrom.

About the translation and the translators

We have for the most part followed the YIVO standard for Yiddish transliteration. Exceptions are Yiddish words that have conventional English spellings. We placed our footnotes and Polish place names that could be identified {in braces}. To improve readability, we added subtitles and occasionally shortened the text.

Robert Brym, FRSC, is SD Clark Professor of Sociology Emeritus and an Associate of the Centre for Jewish Studies at the University of Toronto. His latest works include Robert Brym and Randal Schnoor, eds, *The Ever-Dying People? Canada's Jews in Comparative Perspective* (Toronto: University of Toronto Press, 2023) and "Jews and Israel 2024: Canadian Attitudes, Jewish Perceptions," *Canadian Jewish Studies/Études Juives Canadiennes* (38: 2024), 6–89. For downloads of Brym's published work, visit https://utoronto.academia.edu/RobertBrym.

Eli Jany is a PhD student in the Department of Germanic Languages and Literatures and the Centre for Jewish Studies at the University of Toronto. He has translated poems by Sarah Reisen (*In geveb*, 12 May 2020, https://ingeveb.org/texts-and-translations/three-poems-reisen) and, with Robert Brym, co-translated volume 1 of *The Last Years of Polish Jewry* and "Jewish Economic Life in Yiddish Literature: Yitskhok Ber Levinzon and Yisroel Aksenfeld," *East European Jewish Affairs* (53, 1: 2023), both by Yankev Leshchinsky.

PART 1
POGROMS

1. The pogroms in Poland, 1935–37

Comparative pogromology

Pogroms in each country and era have a unique character and scope, because every pogrom wave has its own driving force, agents, ideologues, perpetrators, and organizers, its own economic basis, political atmosphere, and social environment.

Tsarist pogroms were to a great extent directly organized and executed by state organs.[1] Their socio-ideological environment was the insignificant and uninfluential Black Hundreds,[2] an organization that was sustained by the financial support of the tsarist government. Their political support was from a thin stratum of reactionary monarchist intellectuals. The large, intellectually rich, and influential Russian intelligentsia—from journalists for small provincial newspapers to great men of letters and painters—opposed tsarism, the pogroms, and the entire anti-Jewish policy. Their struggle against tsarism was consequently transformed into a struggle against antisemitism.

The class basis of the tsarist pogroms was very narrow. It consisted of the so-called *meshchantsvo*—urban Christian storekeepers and artisans, the only social groups negatively affected by Jewish competition and capitalist agility, although they feared these talents much more than they suffered from them. All other classes were so caught up with the economic upswing of capitalist Russia and so enchanted with the

---

1 {A more nuanced and now widely accepted account of the first tsarist-era pogroms, placing little emphasis on government initiative and more on the economic and class context, was initiated by I. Michael Aronson, *Troubled Waters: The Origins of the 1881 Anti-Jewish Pogroms in Russia* (Pittsburgh PN: University of Pittsburgh Press, 1990).}

2 {An extreme nationalist and pro-monarchist Russian movement of the early twentieth century.}

struggle to loosen social and national restraints, opening wide doors for young and vigorous Russian capitalism, that, with rare exceptions, there could be no question of students, intellectuals, and the better part of the bourgeoisie participating in pogroms.[3] The Russian bourgeoisie and the intelligentsia—the most important political forces in the country—benefited from blessed Jewish agility because the Jews were the most talented and nimble elements distributing manufactured goods from Moscow and Russian cultural treasures over the length and breadth of the country. They suffered least from Jewish competition because Jews were largely confined to the Pale of Settlement.

The tsarist pogroms were bloody and cruel because they were carried out by mercenary secret agents, ex-police officers, incentivized members of the underworld, and even soldiers in the painfully infamous Bialystok pogrom of 1906 in which as many as 100 Jews were killed, many of them women, children, and the elderly.

The goal of the tsarist pogroms was decidedly political—to drown Bolshevism, which had so quickly captured the hearts of the Ukrainian masses, in Jewish blood; to scare away the Jewish masses from participating in the revolutionary movement; and to divert the rage of the dissatisfied masses from the political regime to the Jewish scapegoat.

The Petliura and Denikin pogroms (1918–1921) were utterly different.[4] In the red-hot atmosphere of war and revolution; in the complicated skein of ethnic and social contradictions that uniquely characterized Ukraine, entangled and deepened by the hunger that the Russian and German armies left as their legacy; in the incandescent atmosphere of the social and ethnic struggles, it was inevitable that the disorganized Ukrainian army regiments and organized adventurist bands would awaken the traditions of the Haidamaks, the slaughter tradition of Khmelnitsky's and Honta's Cossacks.[5] The Ukrainian pogroms were

---

3   {Leshchinsky ignores the important role played by peasants and workers in the tsarist-era pogroms. See Aronson, *ibid.*}
4   {Symon Petliura was Supreme Commander of the Ukrainian People's Army and leader of the Ukrainian People's Republic during the Ukrainian War of Independence/Russian Civil War. Anton Denikin was Deputy Supreme Ruler of the anti-Bolshevik Russian State proclaimed in 1918. Both were implicated in the pogroms that took place between 1918 and 1921.}
5   {Ukraine was colonized by the Polish-Lithuanian Commonwealth (1569–1795). Agricultural estates in the region were controlled by members of the Polish nobility, worked by Ukrainian peasants, and managed largely by Jews, who also monopolized the liquor trade and performed various other middleman functions.

therefore transformed into terrifying mass slaughters with tens of thousands murdered and wounded and hundreds of thousands fleeing their homes.

The goal here was also expressly political—to drown Bolshevism, which had quickly and strongly captured the hearts of the Ukrainian masses, in Jewish blood; discourage the awakened and excited Jewish masses from participating in the political struggle; create a chasm between Jewish and Ukrainian workers; and deflect attention from the class struggle, which the Bolsheviks stressed, to the ethnic struggle.

If the central organizer of the tsarist pogroms was the police department, then it was the general staff in the Petliura pogroms. If in the tsarist pogroms it was necessary to organize pro-pogrom sentiment in every place, then in the time of war and revolution it was enough merely to show the way and pro-pogrom sentiment overwhelmed the entire land like a plague. If in the tsarist pogroms it was enough to kill any Jew to foment panic among all Jews and hold their political activities in check, then in the revolutionary fire of 1918–19 it was necessary to murder young Jewish men, the pogromists' actual or potential political opponents. In the Petliura pogroms, the percent of murdered Jewish men between the ages of twenty and forty-five was therefore shockingly high. There were also slaughters of entire cities and towns where not only elderly people, women, and children were exterminated, but even the sick who were dragged out of hospitals. However, the organizers and ideologues of the Petliura pogroms, the masters of Petliura's general staff, aimed for Jewish youth.

The class basis of the Petliura pogroms was broad, although conditioned by the war and the times. There existed a deep contradiction between the Ukrainian countryside and the towns where Jews lived. The peasants brought grain, eggs, milk, butter, and other products to town but could not sell them for enough money to buy the salt, rolling tobacco, kerosene, matches, and material for clothes that they needed. Jewish storekeepers, who carried all these items in minimal quantities, followed the tradition common to all storekeepers throughout the world and among all peoples; they insisted on extracting the highest

---

Ukrainian uprisings led by Bohdan Khmelnytsky, Ivan Honta, and other Cossacks in the seventeenth and eighteenth centuries involved the slaughter of thousands of Jews, Polish nobles, and Uniates (Eastern Catholics).}

prices possible. The gap between the price of agricultural products and manufactured goods was enormous. Therefore, in the previously described heated atmosphere it was not at all difficult to make the small-town Jewish storekeeper with an inventory worth all of ten roubles that he hoped to sell for a 10% or 20% profit—this small screw in the complicated machine of the war-and-revolution economy—seem responsible for all the war troubles, the mobilizations, requisitions, "contributions," and plain robberies conducted by regular and irregular armies that sprang up like mushrooms after rain and swept the country like locusts. The hungry, war-weary, exasperated Ukrainian peasant eagerly adopted the slogan: release your bitterness on the Jews, the historical scapegoat.

Unique features characterized the Denikin pogroms even though they occurred mainly in the same heated Ukrainian atmosphere. With Great Russian White officers lacking their own national environment and masses—occupiers in essence, threatened from two sides, by the Bolsheviks and the Ukrainians—the Denikin army had to live by robbery.[6] Hatred and contempt toward Jews combined with a special sympathetic weakness for Jewish women were inherited characteristics in this aristocratic-officer environment. Anger against Jews as the most formidable enemies of tsarism was also transmitted from generation to generation. It is therefore no surprise that Jews became the most suitable object for the Denikin pogroms, the main features of which were plunder and rape.

For the sake of their honour, it was also much more acceptable for aristocratic officers to place blame for the decline on the weak Jews rather than confess their own responsibility for the social and political reactionaryism that so frightened off the masses, especially the peasants who had barely managed to reclaim land from the nobility.

In both the Petliura and Denikin cases a vicious cycle was created: the more frequent and murderous the pogroms became, the stronger and larger became the flow of Jewish youth to the Red Army; and the more Jewish sympathies for the Reds grew, the crueller and bloodier the pogroms became. Frightened to death by the rivers of Jewish blood that began to flood tens of Jewish towns, and scared enough to flee to the far corners of the world with every movement of the Petliura or Denikin

---

6 {In this context, "White" means anti-Bolshevik, the Bolsheviks being the Reds.}

army group, the Jewish masses, especially the youth, driven by basic instincts, had one way out: to join the Red Army, receive weapons, and thus hope to save women and children from death by pogrom and fall on the battlefield rather than die in an attic or a cellar.

Class-conscious organized Jewish workers, urban and schooled in Marxism, remained anti-Bolshevik much longer than did non-Jewish workers, who had among them many peasant anarchist rebels. The Jewish population in general, more than half of which consisted of bourgeois elements, suffered much more from Bolshevik requisitions and "contributions" than did the non-Jewish population, among which bourgeois elements amounted to just a few percent. And yet opponents of the Bolsheviks and children of bourgeois Jews who were impoverished by the Bolsheviks ran to the Red Army because they were willing to give all, really everything down to the shirt off their back, to anyone who would undertake the mission of stopping the murderer, tearing the knife from his hand or cutting off the hand entirely. For physical rescue they were willing to sacrifice not only material goods and economic resources, not only social principles and achievements, but also political worldviews and ideological differences.

The Red Army undertook the mission of physical rescue, and one must be objective and admit that it often conducted this mission heroically, which far surpassed the general hatred of a common enemy. Understandably, this further inflamed the passion of Petliura's and Denikin's soldiers; the greater their defeats on the battlefield, the more blood they spilled in the helpless unarmed cities and towns. And it is also understandable that the more that innocent Jewish blood was spilled, the more the Jewish masses ran to the Red Army.

In the pogrom waves of contemporary Poland, the central driving force is direct *economic* competition. The agents and directors of the attacks and excesses are those who are directly interested in getting rid of Jewish competition—those who want to take over the Jewish place in the market or the job in the store, the candidates for the position of the Jewish doctor or lawyer, the children of the broad Polish classes of various social origins who are ready and waiting for vacated Jewish occupations.

The political aspect, the blaming of Jews for Communism, for being enemies of Polish independence, for striving to turn Poland into a Jewish-

Polish state—all these are side issues, additional factors secondary to the main point, the economic struggle, that has taken the form of pogroms, murders, knife attacks, and beatings with wooden sticks visited on those who earlier had a job in trade or medicine. In the Russian and Ukrainian pogroms, the organizers were in a police department or an army general staff, but here in Poland they are in a party headquarters that relies on a large mass of people from various classes, on aristocrats and priests, on the urban bourgeoisie and the majority of the intelligentsia, on *petit bourgeois* storekeepers and craftspeople, and on the large number of today's typical *déclassé* individuals from various social classes. And let us also say openly that in that party there are also not a few workers, although the overwhelming majority, the more politically conscious and active majority of the Polish working class, is organized in the socialist party, which fights energetically against the pogroms and antisemitism.

In Russia and Ukraine, participants in the pogroms were agents of the police who discarded their uniforms, anarchic soldiers and bands, desperate officers who in the revolution lost their army and their inherited aristocratic wealth. In Poland, the participants consisted of a large number of the unemployed or those who had not yet joined the paid labour force, from a student to a janitor's son, from an Orthodox priest's daughter to a chimney sweep, from a former landowner's son to a landless peasant, from an unemployed musician to a tailor's journeyman, from an apprentice lawyer to a street merchant, from a hungry artisan working from home to a sated official who lacks access to jobs for his growing children and believes in securing places for them by driving the Jews out of Poland.

Therefore, in Russia and Ukraine, there were bloody pogroms, mass slaughters, but here in Poland there are sporadic murders, excesses, attacks, knifings, beatings with sticks, and bombs placed in Jewish businesses; there, organized, politically connected, and therefore time-limited incidents with the goal of creating political panic or political isolation, political demagogy or simply political deception; but here in Poland separate, disconnected, widely distributed ambushes and attacks that have an entirely different aim—to remove, chase, force out, compel abandonment of a store, a market job, a workshop, a hospital, or a lawyer's practice. One senses in these ambushes and attacks an organized central force—but a party force that can provide slogans, advice, and means but not police or army forces that can initiate and halt incidents when and how they want.

The class base (or, to put it more crudely, primitively, and therefore accurately, the intestinal base) is here shockingly broad: millions of hungry peasants who have nothing to do in the countryside and who rush like a natural force into the city and urban occupations; small shopkeepers, artisans, and homeworkers; large parts of the bankrupted nobility; ruined formerly well-to-do peasants; urban bourgeois elements suffering from the economic crisis; impoverished intellectuals; and finally, the entire younger generation from all classes and strata, which sees before it no bright prospects in poor Poland, which is pressed between two large economic and political forces—Germany and Russia—and has no room for economic expansion and no hope of political expansion. This broad class basis of antisemitism explains the social atmosphere in which Polish Jewry lives, an atmosphere in which one is suffocated.

Crisis and hunger; overpopulation in the countryside; weak development of industry that cannot absorb the large natural increase of 450,000 people per year; low agricultural prices on the world market; the fall of exports; the decline of emigration, which used to remove 150,000 people a year from the country; and the waning of seasonal labour migration, which used to bring millions of *zloty* into the country annually—all these factors create rich ground for antisemitic agitation and demagogic antisemitic slogans. However, one cannot solve all these serious and complicated economic issues with holes in the skulls of Jewish students and wounds in the breasts of Jewish storekeepers. On the contrary, antisemitic actions further disorganize economic life, which is already minimally organized. They increasingly anarchize certain parts of the population. The panic disturbs the already weak willingness to invest on the part of large sections of the population.

To understand the entire knotted ball of factors that influence Poland's bloodthirsty antisemitism positively and negatively one must consider that the Endek party[7] is the oldest, largest, and strongest antisemitic party in Poland. Although with respect to antisemitism it has brought together enthusiasts and members from all classes and strata, it has not been able to win broad support among the peasantry and working class.

---

7 {The *Narodowa Demokracja* party, widely known as *Endecja* from its abbreviation, ND, founded in 1886.}

It thus remains chiefly a party of the nobility and priests, industrialists and storekeepers, officials and intellectuals. As strongly as this crafty Jesuitical party wants to unite the aristocracy with the peasantry and the industrialists with the workers through antisemitism, it did not and probably will not succeed. This party therefore has broad *socio-political* influence but a small *social* base.

In contrast, the socialist movement, the only organized force that opposes antisemitism in all its forms, has a broad social base—peasants and workers—but a very small political base. That is because the press, the theatre, radio, and all other organs that influence the population, as well as existing political grandstanders, are in the hands of dominant classes that are in Poland without exception antisemitic. Some are for pogroms, others for so-called "cultural" antisemitism, that is, for economic and social antisemitism without bombs and knives. However, practice has already shown that the classes that carry out the antisemitic program, when they write that Jews are the enemies of Poland, that they are harmful to the population, that one must get rid of them as soon as possible and, as long as they are in the country, one must isolate them as much as possible and push them as much as possible into the ghetto, arrive at the only logical conclusion: one must do everything up to and including staging pogroms so Jews will take flight, the faster the better.

One cannot blame the Polish government for organizing pogroms against Jews. However, one can and must blame it for preparing the ground for pogroms: tolerating the propagandizing that inevitably leads to pogroms; allowing to go unpunished the small attacks and casual excesses that whet the appetite of hooligans and that get transformed into mass attacks and killings; and finally, only weakly punishing knifings and murders. In the bitter struggle between right and left, the right throws all its might into concentrating the dissatisfaction of the masses on ethnic antagonism, with the government pouring water on the millstone of this wildly antisemitic right wing. It turns out to be a strange imbroglio. The government, attacked by the Endek party, helps the latter strengthen its position.

In reality, this situation has more to do with political competition. The governing party, *Sanacja*,[8] wants to tear the popular antisemitic

---

8 {*Sanacja*—"sanation" in Middle English—refers to the retroactive validation of an invalid marriage in the Catholic Church. It connotes the healing of Polish social,

slogan out of the hands of the Endek party and use it for its own party interests. However, it lost the competition because, firstly, it was a little late to the game and, secondly, overtaking the Endek party in pogrom agitation and pogrom tactics is in practice exceedingly difficulty. The outcome is fatal. The government isolates the Jews politically, starves them economically, and ghettoizes them culturally, while the Endek party supplements this "state" policy with beatings and killings of Jews, breaking the windows of Jewish houses and throwing bombs into Jewish businesses, driving Jews out of the marketplaces and placing boycott agitators in front of Jewish businesses, setting Jewish homes on fire, and dousing Jewish merchandise with oil. Violent hatred and venomous agitation accompany these actions. If the masses believed one-tenth of the accusations and defamations hurled against the Jews, they would have exterminated all of them long ago.

Let us now turn to the factual part of our work, which will clearly show how tolerant the Polish government is toward the bloodiest antisemitic provocations and pogroms.

The countryside

First, a few words about the material we will use in our work. Unfortunately, it consists only of newspaper articles that have gone through the highly stringent Polish censor, so the articles are like official acknowledgements. In the editorial archives of all Jewish newspapers there are mountains of material that could not be made public due to censorship. This does not mean that the archives do not reflect reality. Quite the opposite. There can be no doubt they were not allowed to be made public because they reflect actual life too clearly. However, we have not used these archival materials.

We begin with the murdered. We have a list with the names of hundreds of murdered people in tens of places. From this alone it is already clear that we are dealing not with bloody mass pogroms but with individual attacks and murders that characterize Polish excesses—

---

economic, and political life. The Sanacja regime assumed power in 1926, when Pilsudski organized an armed coup. Although Sanacja split into totalitarian-nationalist and authoritarian-centrist wings following Pilsudski's death in 1935, it survived until the Nazis occupied Poland in September 1939.}

economic competition with knives and wooden sticks up to the point of murder. Only in Grodno, Pshitik, and Minsk-Mazovyetsk were there real pogroms with the music of breaking glass, feathers flying like snow, human sacrifices, and many wounded in each city.

Let us briefly consider a few terrifyingly characteristic murders. In May 1935, in Duksht {Dūkštas}, Vilna district, a Jewish family—a husband, wife, and children by the name of Feldman—is just about ready to migrate to the land of Israel. They travel to relatives in the neighbouring little town of Vidzi {Vidžiai} to take their leave. They are happy, they are leaving the diaspora, they are going home; the family members have been active Zionists for years. The family is in full harmony; they are in seventh heaven. Friday evening young Yankev Feldman goes for a walk with his relatives on the streets of Vidzi. Suddenly two Christians with whom they are unfamiliar run over to them and deliver blows to the young Feldman's head with pieces of iron and stab his sides with knives. If the hooligans had known this young Jew was willingly about to leave Poland they would certainly have killed someone else because their aim is really not so much to murder as to decrease the number of Jews in Poland.

Here is a murder in the village of Leopoldov in the environs of Shedlets {Siedlce} in June 1935: Goldman, a sixty-two-year-old Jew from Riki {Ryki}, a country merchant, passes by the house of a peasant, Jaras. This peasant's son, a local Endek activist, exits the house with an axe. With its sharp side he splits open the Jew's head. He does not quite kill him because the Jew is destined to writhe in pain for several hours. The Jew dies the next morning in his town while all its Jews cry and lament for Goldman and for the destiny of the entire Jewish community, which finds itself in the line of concentrated Endek fire, accompanied by blood, fear, concerns about tomorrow, and worries about making a living today.

The Jewish community in Minsk-Mazovyetsk was shaken by the murder of Yisroel Tsirlich, a young Jewish man of twenty-odd years, a well-known and beloved local *Po'ale Tsiyon* {Labour Zionist} activist and leader of the party in his city. He came from the train station the Thursday night before the first of May 1936. Suddenly a group of hooligans befell him. They knifed him in the lung and the kidney, having earlier that evening wounded several other Jews on that same road. They left him lying in a pool of blood and ran off. Losing blood, the wounded man barely dragged himself to a Jewish home, but the residents were too frightened by the cries in the street to open the door. He died in the street. Several other Jews were severely wounded that day. Early the next day the hooligans tried to continue their attacks, but they clashed with organized resistance. Two of them were seriously wounded. Several of them were jailed along with the Jewish porter, Yitskhok Ostshega, who was blamed for knifing one of the hooligans.

In the village of Verniki {Zwiernik?} near Pilzne {Pilzno} in Western Galicia lived a Jewish family that owned a store. There was also a non-Jewish storekeeper in the village. In January 1936 the Jewish storekeeper was attacked in an attempted robbery. An eighty-year-old man by the name of Khanine Garlitser and his son were shot and lightly wounded, but this time the attack was repelled. The family remained in the village, living in fear because their enemy, the competitor, threatened and promised revenge. The murderers waited for an evening when both young sons were not in the village and the eighty-year-old remained alone with his daughter. On 20 March 1936 they broke into the store, delivered a blow to the daughter's head with an iron, killing her instantly. Then they broke into the house. The old man was sitting and studying the *gemora*.[9] He hadn't even heard the death-throes of his daughter. They didn't have to struggle long with the old man. One blow of the iron killed him, spraying the *gemora* with blood.

The murder of Jewish landowner Markus Nelken in the village of Rataye {Rataje}, not far from the town of Pizdri {Pyzdry}, was especially shocking. The prelude to the murder involved a Jewish manager who worked for the landowner. The manager's son-in-law, Mordkhe Bararbis, had a small shop in the village, where, in 1935, an Endek organization was formed. From then on, the Jewish storekeeper didn't have a quiet day. In the beginning the Endeks advised him to leave the village but he did not. However, when they started repeatedly breaking the store's windows, he understood the sign of the times and fled.

The antisemitic organization kept on growing. The population was incited. In the village there was frequent discussion of putting an end to the *zhids*.[10] The main role in the organization was played by

---

9 {The second part of the Talmud, consisting of rabbinical analysis and commentary on the first part, the *mishna*.}
10 {*Zhid* is a derogatory term for Jew.}

one Sobolevski and, even more, his wife. Sobolevski worked for a Jew, Nelken, but he spoke not of his Jewish boss but of the *zhid*. A celebration of the patriotic organization's new flag took place, and Sobolevski's wife gave a provocative talk in the church. On 9 March 1936 Sobolevski went to Nelken with an axe under his coat. He delivered two blows to Nelken's head, killing him instantly. The police apprehended Sobolevski only two days later. Bound in chains, he mockingly remarked that he got rid of only one *zhid*.

The extent of the tragedy of Polish Jewry, which becomes more insecure in its physical existence day by day; which feels more and more like it is in an environment that is losing the most elementary human feelings in relation to the Jews; which chokes on its last bit of bread because it knows well that this last bit of bread is the main reason for all the hatred and enormous misfortune—the fathomless depth of the tragedy of a landless people, of a tenant people, appears in the murder of three members of the Florents family in the village of Vala-Kurashava {Wola Kuraszowa}.

A poor Jew with a wife and several children lived there. He was the only storekeeper in the village. In 1935 a revolution took place in the village. Marian Mamchik, the son of a peasant, more educated than his father, a reader of antisemitic newspapers, lacking opportunities for work or a job, opened a little shop. And Marian Mamchik declared with words and with stones, with angry stares and with wooden sticks, that he must remain the only storekeeper in the village because there is no room for two.

The indictment states: "Seven days prior to the murder, on 23 December 1935, Marian Mamchik, the owner of a store in Vala-Kurashava, promised the accused, Kazimierz Marei and Jan Fenatshna, several bottles of liquor for breaking the windows of the store of the Jew, Florents." Here is what happened according to the trial report: "On the night of 30 December a group of nine young peasants headed by the two accused entered the shop of Hirsh Florents and sang traditional Christmas carols. The Jew politely received them, and after the songs were finished offered them cigarettes and candies. Nor was he stingy with money. The group left, and the Florents family went calmly to sleep, not sensing that the misfortune they were about to experience approached with every passing minute.

Around midnight they heard an urgent banging on the door. Hirsh Florents got up first and asked, "Who's there?" However, before he managed to hear the answer the doors to the vestibule were thrown open. Florents then bolted the inner doors behind him. Then, the attackers, with indescribable wildness, ripped off the shutters and the windows and tore into the house. The screams of the attacked were heart-rending. Hirsh Florents managed to flee through a side window to call for help, but none of the peasant neighbours wanted to move until he finally convinced one of them. The help was too late. When they arrived at the house they saw by the pale light of a night lamp Miriam Florents lying on the floor with no sign of life. Near the dead mother, four of her children were lying in a pool of blood.

Fourteen-year-old orphaned Zaynvl survived the ordeal with a broken hand and testified at trial: "After they broke and destroyed everything in the house they ran over to mommy with an axe. She begged for mercy and promised to leave the village. We, the children, were hiding under the bed. However, the murderers dragged us out one by one and hit each one on the head and on the body with a board, then covered our heads with buckets."

The widower and father ended his testimony thusly: "When no help came, I ran back home and found a picture of destruction and murder. My wife was lying there with a cut up face and no sign of life. Ten-year-old Moyshele was lying there with his brain split and a cut up body. His mouth was open, as if he let out a shriek before he died. Beside them, twelve-year-old Malkele lay beaten—she was such a dear child. Only fourteen-year-old Zaynvl and six-year-old Yisroel showed signs of life. I then began running with my last strength to the nearest town and only in the morning returned with a doctor. And that morning I finally left the village."

He left, but a little too late. The lively Jew was late this time and thus paid dearly. At trial Florents said that he was already thinking about leaving the village, but the competitors had no patience. At trial they claimed that they believed that in Poland it was permissible to kill Jews and drive them out. One murderer was sentenced to twelve years in prison and the second to six years. However, the jail sentences will not bring the dead back to life, and six-year-old Yisroel, who remained in a prolonged state of shock, will not recover emotionally. The place was "sanitized," and the newly minted Polish storekeeper can celebrate his victory.

Here is a murder typical of those in the Ukrainian villages: on 15 August 1936, in the village of Tulishkov {Tuliszków}, they broke into the home of Diamand, a farmer, decapitating and cutting up the bodies of the entire family of four souls, then setting the house on fire. The neighbours noticed the fire, put it out, and found the mutilated bodies.

And here is another case that clearly illustrates the situation of the Jews in the countryside: in the village of Tsigane, eastern Galicia, lived a Jewish widow, Roze Kon. She was born in the village and lived there for many years. It is not known when her ancestors settled there but it is possible that they arrived a century or even two centuries ago. The widow had a small food shop and there she toiled. Her old mother and a nine-year-old daughter lived with her.

The local antisemites began tormenting the widow. Pickets outside her store didn't allow Christian customers to enter. There were actually days when they had no income. In the end, antisemites broke in at night and murdered the woman. A local well-known antisemite was arrested and evidence existed that he participated in the murder. The sorrow and despair of the two who remained alive—the old woman and the young daughter—cannot be described.

In the village of Khnidav, eastern Galicia, they murdered the Jew, Yosef Meser, and his wife, Gitl. Both were more than seventy years old and had lived their entire lives in the village. They murdered them with an axe while they were in their beds and then set fire to the beds. In all these cases, nothing was stolen, an indication that the murder was not a result of robbery but was an "ideational," "patriotic" murder.

A Jew was standing in his house in the village of Nove-Myasto {Nowe Miasto} saying his evening prayers. Suddenly a shot rang out. He died on the spot. Who shot him? Why? Nobody was apprehended. We therefore don't know who shot him. However, we know why he was shot. He was a Jew, and that answers all questions.

Frequently one reads in Yiddish newspapers such notices: "On the road near Slonim two dead Jews were found. They used to travel between villages" (*Haynt*, 9 May, 1937). In the period of interest here we counted eight murdered Jews whose names could not be determined. Here is a brief notice typical for murders in Ukrainian villages: "Sunday, 28 March

1937, in the village of Kotlov {Kotłów}, the horrifying murder of Moyshe Kugler and his wife was carried out. After stabbing him with knives, the bandits slit his throat and shot his wife three times. The deceased left three orphans between the ages of eight and fourteen. It is believed that the perpetrators were Ukrainian nationalist terrorists" (*Dos naye vort*, Warsaw, 31 March 1937). And here is another interesting notice: "This evening (5 January 1937), in the village of Maike, Dalhin county, eastern Galicia, three masked bandits entered the apartment of Dovid Klinger and stabbed him and his wife, Gitl, to death with stilettoes. Nothing in the house was disturbed" (*Folkstsaytung*, Warsaw, 7 January 1937).

The declaration a murderer gave in a Lemberg {Lvov; Lviv} court is characteristic of the mood that has emerged in the population. He killed the Fridman couple from Yanov {Janów}, and during the trial said the following: "In the military they taught me that the Bolsheviks are the biggest enemies of the Polish state. Because all Jews are Bolsheviks, I believed I did well by killing a couple. Hitler would have awarded me a distinction" (*Folkstsaytung*, Warsaw, 10 April 1937).

The fatal influence of antisemitic provocation on the population—especially on the rural population, which is much more naïve and often takes the words of a newspaper as a sort of command or recommendation from the regime—was expressed even more clearly during the trial. Consider also the trial of a young peasant from the village of Leshno {Leszno}, near Kozhenits {Kozienice}, who lured two village merchants, Leyb Flamenboym, aged seventy, and Meylekh Goldvaser, aged forty-two, with the proposal to sell them hides, and killed them with a hammer. He was arrested the same day at his friend's wedding. He was led away from the dancing, chained, and jailed. At trial he openly, calmly, and cold-bloodedly declared that he killed the two Jews because he read in the newspapers that the Jews must be driven out of Poland. The prosecutor demanded the death penalty. Frightened by the prosecutor's speech, the murderer, in his last words, appealed to the judges for clemency because he didn't kill actual people, just Jews (*Haynt*, Warsaw, 16 November 1936).

The following case perfectly expresses the atmosphere in which Poland's village Jew lives. The large ten-member Miler family lived in the village of Zhidlovyetz. On the night of 8 June 1937 their house was set on fire. Awakened, the family jumped out of their beds to try and save themselves. However, the doors were securely bolted from the outside by boards. The Millers barely managed to escape, although two family members were badly burned. One of the two, Meylekh Miler, aged thirty, died the same day of his wounds. The newspaper correspondent wrote the following: "Though the Jew got along well with his neighbours—peasants—nobody wanted to give him a ride to the hospital because they feared revenge" (*Folkstsaytung*, Warsaw, 14 June 1937).

The murder of Monish Poznanski from Kviv {Klwów} shows how far the cruelty of the hooligans can reach and how wild the entire population becomes in the pogrom atmosphere. The surviving eight- and thirteen-year-old grandchildren painted a picture of inhumanity that curdles the blood in one's veins.

During a pogrom in Kviv, Jews fled to Pshitik. Children, women, the elderly, the ill, baskets with a few items, featherbeds—all thrown together in wagons, and they flee to blessed Pshitik, which already survived the inevitable pogrom edict. On the way, they threw the Jews out of the wagons and beat them. We let the children tell the rest: "Our grandfather was lying on the ground. There was a large black spot near his temple. We carried him, his arms around us. He didn't speak, and his eyes were bloodshot. We took him to Vozhniak, the school teacher, but Vozhniak locked his door and didn't let us in. We continued over the entire village but nobody wanted to help. They didn't even give us a little water. Our grandfather became weaker and weaker, and he was wobbling. When we arrived at another village, Vzhesub {Wrzeszczów} it was already evening. I took two *zloty* out of grandfather's wallet to hire a wagon to Pshitik. We said to one of the peasants: 'Help us bring our grandfather to Pshitik. He will pay you well. He is a good man.' It didn't help. We had to return to the village of Potvorub {Potworów}, where we went to the village magistrate. Grandfather fell down and started to moan. The magistrate got a wagon and brought us to Pshitik" (*Moment*, Warsaw, 20 July 1937). When they brought the sixty-four-year-old Poznanski to the hospital in Radom, the doctor determined that his eyes had been gouged and his skull fractured. That night, Poznanski died without regaining consciousness.

We will end this chapter of rural hell with the frightful murder of five Jewish souls in the village of Stavi {Stawy}, Kelts district. Here is how the correspondent of a Warsaw newspaper described the murder, which terrified the entire area and filled all the country Jews of the region with indescribable dread (*Folkstsaytung*, Warsaw, 20 October 1937): "Moyshe Shmulevitsh had for many years lived in the village of Stavi and had a little shop there. Recently Shmulevitsh had received threats demanding that he leave the village. At about 11:30 on the tragic Thursday night of 15 October 1936, someone knocked on his door. Shmulevitsh, thinking it was a customer, opened the door. Several men entered and immediately began shooting. The first victim to fall was Moyshe Shmulevitsh, then his thirty-five-year-old wife, Sore Rokhl, and his seventy-three-year-old mother. They cut out the tongue of the grandmother. Hearing the shooting, a twenty-three-year-old cousin, Mirl Koyfman, who was their house guest, ran in. She was immediately shot. Then the teacher, Moyshe Kenigshteyn, was murdered. Only the two children who hid themselves survived: twelve-year-old Yankl and sixteen-year-old Feygele."

To clarify the depth of the tragedy of the rural Jewish population, it is enough to briefly quote from the speech of the attorney for the main defendant in the murder trial, the young peasant, Józef Zhepyetski. Lawyer Tshikhovski exclaimed: "Here is the young Christian village merchant, who yearns for trade. The whole country regards him and such as him with delight; he and such as him should be freed. He is a young productive type and there are many like him in Poland."

All the accused were freed, but in a few months it turned out that this young peasant, whom "the whole country regards with delight," was the murderer not only of the Jewish family but of his friend in crime, whom he began to suspect would betray him.

The cities

The murders described earlier have an avowed economic character. Almost all murders in the countryside must be considered as such. Urban murders have an entirely different character. In the former case Jews are typically murdered by an acquaintance, often a neighbour with whom they had good or bad relations for many years, but in all cases, relations under which lay certain economic interests. The situation is completely different in the latter case. In cities, Jews are attacked and murdered by strangers whom they had never seen before and with whom they had absolutely no prior relations. They are murdered *simply because they are*

Jews, only because they belong to a certain ethnic group. The fatal influence of antisemitic provocation is easily determined in both rural and urban murders, but in the urban murders, members of antisemitic parties are the main perpetrators, often with the direct influence of a party meeting. The direct influence of wild but permitted antisemitic agitation emerges in its naked form in the urban murders. These murders are *political*, not in the sense that the attackers have political accounts to settle with those who were attacked, but in the sense that members of certain parties include murdering Jews in their program. However, not all urban murders have a political character; the impression is created among many urban Poles that one can resolve the problem of Jewish competition with an axe or a revolver.

Here are a couple of examples. On one and the same street in Vilna, Savitsh Street, there lived two shoemakers: a Jew, Simkhe Magid, and a Christian, Franciszek Nikolayev. The former worked in a little shoe factory and the latter had an open workshop. They were of course not well-to-do; the factory worker was doubtless poorer than the owner of his own workshop. The Jew lost his job when the little factory closed. He was weeks without income. They eat up everything they have left, pawn their last few pillows, and then he, his wife, and their five-year-old son go hungry. Magid decides to open a workshop, like thousands of the unemployed do everywhere. He borrows and scrapes together a few tens of *zloty* and opens a workshop facing the street. The Christian doesn't think long. He takes a hammer, tears into Magid's workshop, and delivers several blows to his head. This is not the place to describe the suffering of the poor shoemaker, who lost his ability to speak, then his eyesight, and died two days later (*Folkstsaytung*, Warsaw, 14 August 1937).

Here is a second case, deriving not from the competitive struggle but simply from the lawlessness that exists when one buys from a Jew. In the town of Stanin, Lukov {Łuków} county, there was a fair, where a Jewish hat maker worked. A peasant went to him for a hat. He tried on hats until one appealed to him. He put the hat on his head and walked away. The Jews ran after him and asked to be paid, and the peasant paid him right there by hitting him on the head with a wooden peg. The Jew fell in a puddle of blood and died before being brought to the hospital (*Folkstsaytung*, Warsaw, 20 June 1937).

Let us turn now to political murders, not in the sense that members of various political orientations struggle against one another and their struggles reach the point of reciprocal murder, but in the sense that, in this case, every Jew, old or young, devout or not, conservative or radical, is regarded as an enemy who deserves the death penalty.

Fig. 4 Members of the Bund marching on 1 May 1936, Warsaw. ©Yad Vashem Photo Archive, Jerusalem, archive item 1605_626, https://photos.yadvashem.org/photo-details.html?language=en&item_id=10143&ind=3

The most outrageous murder that terrified not just the Jewish population but also large parts of better Polish society was that of a five-year-old Jewish child at the Bund[11] demonstration on 1 May 1937. Members of the Nara Party {*Obóz Narodowo-Radykalny*, the National Radical Party} shot into the Jewish crowd that stood on the sidewalk and watched the demonstration. They released a thick volley of fifty to sixty revolver shots and threw several petards. One can imagine what kind of panic

---

11 {The General Jewish Labour Bund in Poland was an offshoot of the General Jewish Labour Bund in Lithuania, Poland, and Russia. It was formed in 1914 when Poland came under German control and contact with Russia became difficult. It won a majority of votes for Jewish parties (nearly 62%) in the 1938–39 election. Antony Polonsky, "The Bund in Polish Political Life, 1935–1939," in *Essential Papers on Jews and the Left, ed. by* Ezra Mendelsohn (New York: New York University Press, 1997), pp. 166–97.}

such an attack can elicit. Victims were numerous. In the crowd stood a mother with her five-year-old son in her arms. One child, one eye in one's head.[12] A bullet hit the child, little Avremele Shaynker, in the temple. He died immediately. Fifty-year-old Feyge Nivan and her husband lay in blood. She was hit by three bullets in her stomach, foot, and hand. Hersh Drumlevitsh, a forty-three-year-old shoemaker, was wounded in a cheek and an eye. Lightly wounded were fifty-nine-year-old merchant, Avrom Englisher, eight-year-old Gershn Perlmuter, a sixteen-year-old Nisnboym and a few others. People who had no connection with the demonstration therefore suffered.

A few days later, the heroes of the Nara Party put out a flyer in which they expressed pride in having attacked Jewish "Marxism." However, even this vile justification does not correspond to reality. For the Nara people, all Jews are Marxists, all Marxists are Jews, and five-year-old Avremele Sheynker, whose childish eyes were so delighted by a Jewish May Day demonstration, was certainly a candidate "Marxist."

No less frightful and also no less vile and cowardly was the murder of a couple of Jews in Lodz {Łódź}. In September 1936, the Polish Socialist Party commemorated the thirtieth anniversary of "Bloody Wednesday," a day when the party carried out an armed attack on the bloody Tsarist police force in 1906.[13] The Lodz branch organized a large demonstration. The *boyovke* {combat unit} of the Nara party organized an attack on the demonstration, but came out of it badly because the socialist militia rebuffed them. Unable to engage in an open fight with the socialist militia, they sought an easier way to release their built-up patriotic energy. They went to Jewish streets and started breaking windows and heads. One of the passers-by, a Jew by the name of Glitsenshteyn, forty-four years old, was stabbed by a Nara man while exiting a streetcar and died on the spot. There were many other Jewish wounded. One cannot deny that Jews are responsible for Polish socialists commemorating the Polish struggle against the tsar; Jews played a big role in Bloody Wednesday, unfortunately not only as subjects, as active organizers and participants in the fight against the tsar, but also as objects because the tsarist regime also compensated Jews with pogroms for their participation in the Polish freedom struggle. In this manner, Polish Jews were paid twice with

---

12 {From the Yiddish saying, "One guards a child like an eye in one's head."}
13 {Congress Poland was under Russian control.}

pogroms for their participation in the Russian revolutionary struggle, once by the tsar before the freeing of Poland and a second time by the Nara Polish patriots after the freeing of Poland.

The commemoration of the struggle against the tsar cost the Jews of Lodz dearly, but Jews in other Polish cities paid no less. In Warsaw, the Lodz scenario repeated itself. The Nara members attacked the socialist demonstration and had to retreat under attack and in disgrace. Having withdrawn from a strong opponent, they turned to a weaker "enemy"— the Jew. They took to the streets and beat every Jew they met and broke every Jewish window, and ambulances picked up the wounded: Yitskhok Goldman, aged fifty-six; Avrom Diamant, aged twenty-two; Ben-Tsien Marienshtat, aged fifty-four; Henek Lebenboym, aged twenty-one; Yisroel Berezniak, aged thirty; Dovid Vofshnit, aged twenty-one; and Yankev Gotfrid, aged twenty-one. These are the wounded who were registered, but as a general rule that we have confirmed many times, the non-registered wounded are at least three times as numerous.

On 30 January 1937 the official Polish telegraphic agency announced: "On 27 January this year on Pomorska Street three citizens of the Jewish faith were attacked and wounded or killed—Grinshteyn, Fishl; Khelmner, Shimen; and Tshariski, Fayvl. Khelmner died of his wounds. The authorities managed to arrest the murderer, twenty-five-year-old Jan Antczak, a commander in the National Radical Party's militia. The murder was executed with a Finnish knife."

Did the murderer have an unsettled account with the patriotic commander? Yes, a large unsettled account, although they had never laid eyes on one another. This is how the matter unfolded. On the evening of the 27th, in the National Radical Party meeting hall, the renowned priest, Trzeciak, made a presentation stating that all the misfortunes of Poland, both historically and at present, derive only from the Jews. If Jews were not in Poland, the country would be rich and powerful. Well, a Polish patriot, especially one who occupies such a high position as commander of the militia, will understandably want to free the fatherland of its enemies. So Anczak leaves the party meeting and immediately begins fighting against the enemies of the fatherland. Khelmner died, and was therefore entirely vanquished, and several others were badly wounded, and therefore only partly vanquished, but they at least became less harmful.

This commander was accused of the murder of two Jews, and it is worthwhile to consider his trial for a moment because it indicates the atmosphere in which such murders became not just possible but inevitable. First, the indictment stated that "Glitsenshteyn was murdered in a beastly manner. He was already lying dead on the streetcar tracks while Anczak kept on striking his head with an axe until the head became a formless bloody mass of flesh."

In response to the judge's question as to whether he admitted killing the two Jews, Anczak joyously answered: "Yes, the Jews are spies, harmful people; at the demonstration they shouted anti-Polish and anti-religious slogans." The judge: "Why did you kill Glitsenshteyn? He wasn't even at the demonstration." The accused: "But he is also a Jew." To the judge's question of whether the accused saw Glitsenshteyn's open skull, Anczak responded: "Yes, I saw that. Afterwards I calmly left. This is what one must do!" (*Folktsaytung*, Warsaw, 22 May 1937).

Here is how Jews fall from murderous hands *because they are Jews* and because a party that openly preaches on behalf of the murder and extermination of Jews and that arms its members operates legally. On 9 November 1936 someone suddenly started breaking the windows of Yosef Berkovitsh's little shop at 11 Kilinskogo {Kilińskiego} street in Lodz. Not every Jew is terrified by every bang on a window. The owner of this shop went out and ran after the person who broke the windows. The vandal immediately pulled out a revolver and started shooting Jews who had meanwhile assembled. Two Jews—Berkovitsh and Zendl—were so badly wounded that they died the next day. Two other Jews, Mendl Rubenshteyn and Moyshe Vayszam, were also badly wounded but remained alive. The question remains as to whether their survival will be enjoyable. Who was the shooter? An eighteen-year-old youth, Tadeusz Shanyavski, in whose pocket a National Radical Party membership card was found (*Nayer Folks-blat*, Lodz, 10 November, 1937).

To convey the mood of the Jewish population in these murderous days is impossible. Tens of thousands of Jews took part in the funeral processions, led by representatives of the *kehila*.[14] They protested and cried, fainted and demanded physical defence against the hooligans,

---

14 {A *kehila* is a Jewish community, especially an organized Jewish community, not to be confused with a *kahal*, the council responsible for community decision making.}

who were openly armed and openly incited to commit murder. Panic encompassed the Jewish population, and mothers were afraid to let their children out on the streets.

The same type of murder also occurred in Kalisz, where two Polish youngsters, one eighteen and the other fourteen, murdered a seventeen-year-old Jewish boy, Manyek Kronenberg. They confessed that they did not know him and had never before seen him, but they frequented the party office, where they heard much talk about Jews as the worst enemies of Poland, and they wanted to accomplish something, so they stabbed the first Jew they encountered.

Such "political" murders numbered forty or fifty in the last two years. We will not recount each one. However, it is a moral obligation at least to recall the fallen member of the {Zionist} Pioneers group, Fride Volkoviska, eighteen years old, who was shot through a window of the Pioneers house on their farm in Grokhov {Grochów} near Warsaw. It was determined that the murder was executed by a member of the National Radical Party.

We noted earlier the poisoned atmosphere in which rural Jews lived. Let us now provide an example showing how far the wildness reached in the cities. In July 1936, not far from Warsaw, near Shvider {Świder}, two Jews were swimming, a young man by the name of Hokhman and a young woman, Fridman. They both began to drown. She managed to reach the shore but the young man died. The young woman related that the whole time some Christians stood on the shore and heard the shouts of Hokhman, who struggled for an entire quarter of an hour with the waves, calling out and begging for help—but the Christians laughed and said: "Let there be one less Jew."

We will later deal more precisely with antisemitic occurrences in many Polish cities that must be referred to by their proper name: pogroms. However, one defining feature of the tsarist pogroms, and certainly a very important one, is absent from the Polish pogroms—the number of casualties is relatively small, and in some pogroms no one was killed. That is true, at least, if we count deaths at the time of the pogrom itself. If one counts deaths including the number of people who were wounded during a pogrom and later died, the picture changes a little.

For example, the Brisk pogrom of May 1937 almost became best known for the fact that after sixteen hours of rampaging, pillaging, and beating, there was not one Jewish death but tens of wounded and hundreds of robbed stores. Some Polish newspapers that preach "cultural" antisemitism even expressed pride in the "humanism" of the Polish pogromists. In reality, this "humanitarian" pogrom entailed three or four Jewish deaths. We will soon explain the "or," but first we turn to the three certain Jewish deaths.

Borekh Zilberberg, a forty-seven-year-old Brisk resident, had a watchmaking business at 41 Dombrovski {Dąbrowskiego} Street. During the pogrom they broke into his shop and beat him over the head with sticks. He suffered a stroke. He was taken to Warsaw, where he was operated on several times, but the operations were unsuccessful. On 29 May, after two weeks of inhuman suffering, he died. The authorities did not allow the body to be brought to Brisk or buried in Warsaw during daytime. At 3 a.m., when the city was fast asleep, they had to bury the body of the first victim of the Brisk pogrom. Only three of Zilberberg's brothers and his wife were present. His wife fainted repeatedly.

A week later, the Jews of Brisk carried the second pogrom victim to their own cemetery: Lutenberg, a fifty-year-old tailor. During the pogrom they executed a real massacre at the poor tailor's place. They shattered two of his sewing machines, tore up the bedding, broke the furniture, cut up everything he has working on, including a pair of officer's pants, and smashed his head with a stone. We mention the stone last because, for a couple days, Lutenberg lamented his broken sewing machines more than the injury to his head. But the morning after the pogrom festival it was necessary to supply his wife and children with bread. A few days later he lay down, and in three weeks he gave up his soul to God.

Only four months later did another Brisk resident die—fifty-year-old Khaim Perlis. He, too, was beaten about the head with stones and sticks. He hung on for four months, but did not manage to twist out of the hands of the Angel of Death.

And here is the fourth of the "three or four" deaths mentioned earlier. During the pogrom, a Mrs. Grinberg was struck in the head with a piece of iron. Her skull was cracked and they barely managed to save her by sewing up her wounds. In a few weeks her condition worsened and she was operated on in Warsaw. She remained alive. But was she not jealous of her pogrom colleagues who had already been relieved of their suffering? Were the previously mentioned Brisk pogrom victims luckier than their colleagues in Pshitik who died on the spot and did not have to endure hellish brain operations, flickering for weeks before dying?

The same was the case for the victims of other "bloodless" pogroms. A whole year after the Minsk-Mazovyetsk pogrom, one of its victims, thirty-one-year-old Khaim Shimenovski, died in a Warsaw hospital. During the pogrom he was hit in the head with a stick and from then on he suffered until he died on 30 May 1937. The Grodno Jew, Leyb Shapiro, lay tormented in hospital for one-and-a-half years after receiving several head and chest wounds during the Grodno pogrom.

And the Pshitik pogrom? Everyone knows about the Minkovskis' cruel murder. In addition, an entire family was killed, their deaths mentioned only in the official chronicle.

During the pogrom, shoemaker Gedalye Tishler hid with his adult children in his attic but the hooligans found them there and dealt them murderous blows with sticks. All of them were wounded, but not seriously. In any case, for a few days nobody could predict that in half a year the members of this family would be dead. At first, the daughter, twenty-three-year-old Feyge, died. Soon after, the twenty-two-year-old son, Yudl, met the same fate. And a few months later, the father died. The widowed mother prays for death because she has been left not only forlorn, broken, and psychologically ruined, but also physically weak and with absolutely no material means with which to live. To live?... Is this living? Is it not easier for those who had the good fortune to lose the world at the first blow to the head?

Not all residents of Pshitik are so unfortunate as to linger years before their redemption from life in the diaspora. Here is a lucky resident by the name of Den who did not suffer from the Pshitik pogrom—but was destined to die at the hands of a pogromist from Pshitik. Fate caught up with him in Radom, where the victims of the Pshitik pogrom lie. On 15 March 1937 he passed by the building where the infamous Pshitik trial took place. Den instinctively stopped. What sort of Jew could pass by the Polish courthouse where for the first time in independent Poland a verdict was reached that punishes those who defended themselves and frees those who beat and murder? Suddenly he heard a tearful cry from a Jew. A well-known pogromist from the Pshitik area, Stanislav Simtshik, was beating a Jew, a fruit merchant, seventy-year-old Yankev

Ayznberg. Den started running over to Ayznberg but didn't manage to get all the way there because the pogromist turned around and delivered a blow to his head with a stick. The blow was such that Den never regained consciousness and died a few hours later. A month later a short letter from his widow was published in the Jewish press: "My children and I are simply dying from hunger. Maybe good people will be found who can help us. Feyge Khaye Den." We include Den as a victim of the pogroms for two reasons—first, because he was killed by an active pogromist from Pshitik, and second because if he had not been standing by the building in which the Pshitik trial took place, he would have perhaps avoided being killed.

We have so far discussed victims who to varying degrees were direct victims of attacks. However, there were no fewer indirect victims as a result of the pogrom atmosphere and especially pogrom fear. For example, there was a pogrom in November 1936 in Vilna. It was one of those pogroms that supposedly demonstrated the higher culture of the Polish pogromists, who are said not to murder as energetically as their tsarist or Petliura colleagues did. How should we categorize the death of the following Jewish victim? On 20 November 1936, National Radical Vilna students organized a prayer meeting in a church. The bishop blessed them. After prayers, and laden with the Bishop's blessing, they let loose in the streets beating Jews and breaking windows. The seventy-year-old Jew, Borekh Feldsher, was walking in the street. Out of fear, he had a heart attack and died on the spot before the blessed students were able to approach him. Was he not a pogrom victim?

The mass pogroms: Grodno, Pshitik, Minsk-Mazovyetsk, Adzhival, 1935–36

In 1935–36 three large pogroms occurred in Poland: in Grodno, June 1935; in Pshitik, March 1936; and in Minsk-Mazovyetsk, June 1936. We view these three events as pogroms in the sense that they involved mass suffering and mass participation in the attacks and murders. Actually, one can speak of a mass-pogrom in one other place, because in Adzhival the attacks and murders of November 1935 had a mass character.

In Poland the attacks have persisted for years. They do not everywhere have the character of mass stands against Jews but of partisan excesses against a few Jews, a few stores, or a few fairs. The attackers do not always have the aim of murder. Sometimes their aim is more to frighten, elicit panic among Jews, and disorganize them, forcing them to run away and emigrate. Therefore, it is very difficult to distinguish between true pogroms and excesses. However, it is in the nature of small-scale pogroms to be transformed into mass events.

Until a certain time, the policy of the government was clear: tolerate a few small pogroms as a good way to assist its entire anti-Jewish economic policy. Make the air suffocating for the Jews, but don't allow mass pogroms that would interest the outside world in the condition of the Jews in Poland. However, it seems that in the last few months the tactics changed and bigger pogroms are now tolerated, but only with beatings and robberies without serious physical injuries. This may be a clearly thought-out plan to let the Jewish and also the non-Jewish world know that there is no longer a place in Poland for the Jews. Emigration is the only escape. This became the *idée-fixe* of leading Polish figures; all means became kosher. One can believe that if mass pogroms without many deaths don't work and the Jews remain stubborn, they will turn to pogroms on the Ukrainian model with mass slaughter.

Let us consider the three large pogroms in chronological order. In doing so we will endeavour to consult the indictments that are certainly not inclined to take the Jewish side. We begin with Grodno, allowing the indictment to trace the evolution of the pogrom:

> In Grodno on the evening of 7 June 1935, there took place the funeral of seaman Kushtsh, who was wounded on 5 June by Shmuel Shteyner and Meylekh Kantarovski during an argument in a dance class. (Both Jewish youth were convicted by the Grodno area court, one sentenced to 12 years and the other to 2 years in prison.) Apart from family, friends, and acquaintances, the approximately 1,000 people who were then in the street attended the funeral. On the way to the cemetery the procession grew steadily, approaching 2,000 people by the time it reached the military cemetery. After the funeral a crowd of close to 1,000 people let loose. It was led by the student, Sunak. Panasiuk, Martshintshuk, Zigmanski, and Zhukovski riled up the crowd. The police told the crowd to disperse, but Panasiuk gave a speech in which he said: "'We have buried a friend whom Jews slaughtered. We must seek revenge for his death! Down with the Jews! Death to the Jews!" Then came the response from the crowd: "Down with the Jews! Beat Jews so that great Poland will live!" Panasiuk shouted: "We already have three facts in Grodno. In 1930 Jews murdered

Moravski, and this year they killed a peasant from Martshinkan and Kushtsh. Tomorrow they will do the same to us! Enough fine words! We need to take action! Let us go to town and show what we can do."

Seeing that Sunak was arranging the crowd in rows, Panasiuk shouted out: "Guys, come with me to beat Jews and avenge the death of our friend! For one of ours, a *hundred* Jews!" This exhortation mobilized the crowd, which set off to the city, tearing out fence posts and collecting cobblestones along the way. Led by the five men mentioned earlier, the mob set off by way of Skidler Street, Yeruzalimska Street, Brigidska Street, Batori Place, Dominican Street, Kalushinska Street, and Napoleon Street, breaking the windows of Jewish stores and dwellings, and beating Jews whom they encountered. The excesses continued from 6:30 to 10 p.m. Around midnight they moved to the suburbs.

During the excesses against Jews the following participants were detained and identified: Olga Zhuk, who broke windows on Yeruzalimska Street; and Kozlovski, who egged on a group of about 100 men to beat Jews and break windows. On Brigidska Street the police detained Mazhdzher, who held a stick and yelled, "Beat Jews," and on Vitoldove Street they detained Balitzki on whom they found a stiletto. While taking him to the police station he resisted arrest. On Kalushinska they apprehended Aleshtshik. His hands were bloodied. With a larger group he had been knocking out windows. On Napoleon Street Yarashevitsh and Romantshuk had been breaking windows. The main leader, Panasiuk, fled. However, on the 17th he gave himself up to the police and confessed.

During the excess the lightly and heavily wounded Jews included Yisroel Berezhinski, Yitskhok Leypunski, Hirsh Grinblum, Iser Atlas, Frantshishek Kovalski, Shmuel Kleynbart, Ber and Avrom Burde, Gotlib Levin, Yankev Gradunski, Gedalye Bekher, Leyb Butshinski, and Shloime Pozniak. Berezovski and Bekher died of their wounds. The inquiry ascertained that windows had been knocked out of 183 houses and eighty-five stores. Damages totalled about 30,000 *zloty*. Trials concerning theft and robbery of property during or immediately after the excesses (there were more than ten of the latter) were transferred to the municipal court or were the subject of separate inquiries.

Of the seventeen accused Poles, only Panasiuk and Plotzki confessed during the inquiry. The others denied participating in the events. The prosecution summoned seventy witnesses to the trial.

According to the indictment, thirteen Jews were wounded, two of whom died. In reality, many more were wounded. Forty people, most of them lightly wounded, were registered in the *kehila*. The number of those who suffered materially was also greater than stated. Three hundred people registered in the *kehila* as having suffered material damages valued in total at more than 60,000 *zloty*. However, it is actually not possible to quantify the bodily and material damage of a pogrom. The shoemaker Gotlib Levin lay in hospital for seven days. The typesetter Leyb Butshinski took seven weeks to heal in Grodno and Warsaw. It is difficult to say whether they fully recovered and their capacity to work was fully restored. Every pogrom leaves an imprint lasting years on reciprocal relations between Jews and Christians, on the mood of the Jewish masses and their sense of security, and on Jewish participation in social and political life.

Grodno had never experienced a pogrom before. For many years, Jews composed a majority of the population, and only in independent Poland did their percentage begin to fall—from 60% in 1897 to 54% in 1921 to 42% in 1931. The Polish population grew proportionately, and with it elements that charged into the mercantile and artisanal livelihoods that had been in Jewish hands for centuries. Polish officials and members of the free professions grew in number even more quickly. These were the two occupational sectors that were the most active bearers and disseminators of antisemitism in Poland.

The trial concerning the Grodno pogrom that took place in November 1935 first uncovered the entire dirty pus that spurted from the infected antisemitic abscess. Aside from one worker who regretted his actions and sought forgiveness, all of the accused vehemently denied everything or audaciously and explicitly declared that they had no regrets, that they had to take revenge, and that they would continue the struggle against the Jews by all available means.

A scene took place that shocked everyone in court. A twelve-year-old orphan, Yosef Blekher, testified that he was standing near his home when his father (a poor tailor who had worked hard for a piece of bread his entire life) was cruelly murdered in the middle of the street, his head beaten until he fell, bloody and unconscious. After this scene, which really shocked everyone in the court, the prosecutor asked the main defendant, Panasiuk, if he regretted his actions. The answer was savage and clear: *he had no regret, he said; the Jews got off easy*. But what can one expect from the Panasiuks and their friends when the lawyers themselves made far more terrifying speeches in court openly calling for the Jews to be rooted out and for the struggle against the Jews to continue by the same means that Panasiuk and his friends used?

By the time of the trial there were already in Grodno three pogrom victims—Moyshe Lipski, Yisroel Berezovski, and Gedalye Bekher. More than ten Jews were seriously wounded and crippled and more than thirty others were lightly wounded, which ruined tens of families and created a pogrom mood in the city for months and perhaps years. How did the court punish the hooligans? Here is the verdict:

- Six accused (Zhukovski, Yudzhak, Baletski, Maleiko, Nobeykon, and Losate) were *freed*.

- Seven accused (Mozedzhezh, Zhukov, Bielski, Aleshtshak, Yaroshevitsh, Romantshuk, and Plotzki) received *six months in jail*.

- Three accused (Kozlovski, Martshintshuk, and Zigmanski) received *nine months in jail*, and the main accused at trial, Panasiuk, received the most severe punishment, just *one year in jail*.

- Nine of the tried men had their sentences delayed for five years.

- Panasiuk and Zygmanski were freed on bail of 200 *zloty* each.

This verdict instilled fear in the Jewish population—not only in Grodno—and deeply upset all Polish Jews. And not only Jews. Grinyevitsh, the Chairman of the court in the Grodno trial (and vice-Chairman of the Grodno regional court), entered a "Votum Separatum." We consider it important to provide the conclusions of this historical document, the contents of which strongly object to the court's verdict:

1. "Such occurrences," the Votum Separatum says, "are a blow to the foundations of legality in Poland. They lower our country in the public opinion of the civilized world.

2. "State power should cut off excesses at their roots without pity. Courts must punish the guilty to the fullest extent of the law.

3. "Weak punishment can only contribute to the audacity of people like Panasiuk and his friends, creating among them a sense of inappropriate defence by the state in connection with the lives and property livelihoods of Jews.

4. "The bearing of the accused in court is a demonstration of their considerable ill will.

5. "The assertion of one witness that on the second and third day after the events Jewish youth began to organize fighting groups with the aim of revenge is an ungrounded supposition because they did not organize for the sake of revenge but for self-defence in case the events recurred.

6. "The responsibility of the accused is not lessened by the claim that their actions were an expression of anger generated by the murder of Christians. Panasiuk and his friends must well understand and remember that in a lawful regime one can punish only those who are directly responsible [for a crime], and punishment is solely the responsibility of the court."

For all these reasons, Chairman Grinyevitsh held that Panasiuk should be imprisoned for three years rather than one year; Kozlovski, Martshintshuk and Zigmanski for two years instead of nine months; and the remaining seven defendants, one year apiece instead of six months.

It must be noted that, a few months after Panasiuk was freed, he placed a bomb in the clinic of the Grodno Society for Safeguarding the Health of the Jewish Population.[15] It caused only material damage, but only because it exploded before opening hours. If it had exploded half an hour later, there would have been many victims.

One must also add that at the appeal trial in Vilna in May 1936, even more severe punishments were handed out than those recommended in the Votum Separatum of the Chairman of the Grodno court: Panasiuk got five years rather than one year, Kozlovski, three years rather than nine months, and Martshintshuk and Zimanski two years instead of nine months, with the sentences of the rest remaining the same. In the end, however, the pogromists were placed in the category of *political activists*,

---

15 {Established in Warsaw in 1921, the *Towarzystwo Ochrony Zdrowia Ludności Żydowskiej* used membership fees and local and foreign donations to protect the health of the country's Jews.}

and amnesty for political criminals was granted to all those sentenced.

If the Grodno pogrom struck like a bolt from the blue because the Jewish population did not take the local Endek organization seriously enough, the same cannot be said for the other pogroms. In Adzhival, Pshitik, and Minsk-Mazovyetsk, the pogroms were the high point of terrorist campaigns that had raged for months in the surrounding region. These anti-Jewish terrorist campaigns caused many wounded in Adzhival, Pshitik, and surrounding towns, and even one murder in Minsk-Mazovyetsk (of Yisroel Tsilikh) before the pogroms. Around Pshitik, the Endek party concentrated a force that was supposed to clear Jews out of a district of about ten towns and provide an example of how to do without Jews in both buying and selling. This pogrom campaign in Adzhival brought about unrest of such proportions that the police had to shoot and kill eighteen peasants. Several police officers were also killed. The number of wounded on both sides was much larger.

The Adzhival pogrom wave is well described in the indictment read at trial in June 1936. We will therefore let the indictment speak for itself even though it greatly minimizes Jewish human and material losses. However, it describes well the entire hellish atmosphere created in the Jewish population and strikingly depicts the demagogic and criminal work of the Endek party, which invented the vilest defamations and wildest fantasies to rile people up against Jews. Unintentionally, the indictment read at trial also offers a splendid picture of what letting pogrom agitation loose can precipitate and how difficult it is afterwards to oppose a mass of people who are freely allowed to be provoked and incited to violence.

Twenty peasants were brought to trial for beating Jews, robbing them, and resisting police. The indictment describes the events thusly:

> Vigorous activity on the part of the Endek party in the territory of Ossa and neighbouring townships dates from 1935. The Endeks engaged in such an extensive propaganda and recruitment campaign among the peasants that in many cases the entire adult population of a village belonged to the Endek party. The economic crisis in the countryside created fertile ground for agitation that was strengthened by demagogic, anti-Jewish slogans and that saw in the Jews the sole reason for every evil in Poland. Together with the development of the Endek organization there took place a boycott that involved not buying and preventing others from buying from Jews. This agitation was at first quiet and restrained.

Later, with the growth of political circles and the recruitment of the masses to the ranks of the Endek party—including irresponsible people, often with a criminal past—recruitment got out of hand and agitation became sharper and took on violent forms, leading inevitably to anti-Jewish excesses.

On Wednesday, 20 November 1935, members of the Endek party in Adzhival, who were assembled in their headquarters, went to the market where a fair was taking place. They formed groups that began walking around the market demanding that the people who were circulating among the stalls and tables not buy from Jews given that the same goods could be purchased from Christians. Clusters of people assembled around these groups, and at a certain moment, due to the pushing of the masses, they began knocking over the Jewish stalls. A group of 30–40 men tipped over the wagon of the Jew, Aleshitski, thereby breaking some of the dishes it contained, and Aleshitski himself was badly injured.

Other groups placed themselves near the Jewish shops. Some went inside, asked to see merchandise, and walked off with it without paying. Merchants who demanded payment were beaten....The merchant Yankl Baritski was hit in the stomach by a stone, and Alter Veksler was hit twice in the face, loosening some of his teeth. Veksler's wife ran after the assailant and stopped him, but he pushed her away. His confederates proceeded to encircle and beat her.

On the following market day, 27 November 1935, similar excesses took place in similar circumstances, the only difference being that they did not overturn Jewish stalls because the Jewish merchants, afraid of what might happen, did not set up their stalls. On that day, directly after a meeting at the Endek local party headquarters, party members began shutting down Jewish stores and beating Jews.

A group of 150 men entered Moyshe Kutshinski's mill, threatening and forcing the peasants who were there to remove the grain they had delivered. They broke the sluices, drained the water, and shut down the mill. They beat the Jews, Khaim Lenge, Meyer Nayberg, Khaim Mlinkevitsh, Yehoyshue Milshteyn, Hershl Leyb Groskop, Leye Fayfer, and Itsik Baritski. With sticks and stones they broke the windows of the houses of Laye Fayfer, Peysekh Rosneholts, Chaim Lenga, Yosl Lerman, and Avrohom Karkovski. While shutting down the stores a few participants beat the Jew, Abram Vayntroyb.

...This time too, although the patrol had been reinforced and numbered eight police officers, because of the aggressiveness of the masses they could not control the situation unless they used guns. So they adopted a wait-and-see attitude, observing the most active individuals who were already known from the events of 20 November: Antoni Grushetzki, Yuzef Khrobak, Pyotr Vzhaski, and Adam Bartos from the village of Asa, as well as Stanislav Grushetski from the village of Zarki, Yan Dzhuba and Zhembitski from Byelin. The last named, armed with a threshing flail, took part in beating many Jews, and Yan Dzshuba threw a stone that hit Baritski's foot.

The two outbreaks in Adzhival were repeated in Pshiskhe on 28 November 1935, and according to available information excesses were also being prepared in other places. This situation threatened the social order, so security forces were compelled to act forcefully against the people whose activities were liable to endanger it. On the evening of 29 November 1935, several members of the Endek party in Adzhival were arrested on suspicion of provoking antisemitic excesses. Then the members of the aggressive party came out against the police decree and sent envoys to the neighbouring villages.

Shortly afterwards, groups of peasants were drawn to Adzhival. Most were armed with sticks, some with pitchforks, axes, and the like. At about nine o'clock Adzhival was surrounded on all sides by a mass of peasants. The inquiry later determined that Endek envoys and "runners" had sounded the alarm to the population of the neighbouring villages. Those who did not want to join the march on Adzhival were terrorized and forced to do so, so only a small number of adult men in a whole series of villages covering a radius of eight kilometres succeeded in remaining in place.

To rile up the masses, a rumour was spread that Jews in Adzhival had arrested Bishop Sandomirski, who was staying there on 28 November, that Jews were torturing priests, and also that the police in Adzhival are in fact not police but Jews dressed in police uniforms. Among the provocateurs only a few people were successfully identified because in most cases an unidentified person rode through the villages on a horse alarming the peasants and telling them to go to Adzhival.

The assembled groups around Adzhival did not dissipate following the police demand, instead assaulting the police with jeers, contempt, and threats. Having an order not to allow the mass into Adzhival, the police repelled the peasants many times and fired warning volleys. However, at certain points this did not work and the situation became more dire. Arms were used, wounding and killing some peasants.

This long excerpt from the indictment demonstrates clearly that the Jewish population was abandoned. For two days the masses rioted, beat, robbed, and destroyed Jewish property while the police "observed" and "registered." No wonder these masses, drunk with plunder, did not believe that the real police opposed them but instead believed that Jews were dressed as police. Above all, this document is witness that the government itself allowed the Endek party to exercise such enormous power over the peasant masses that they could be made to believe the most improbable and absurd accusations, including that the Jews had arrested the bishop and were torturing priests. The indictment does not relate that Poznanski, a sixty-four-year-old local resident, was killed by the same band that organized the pogrom in Adzhival. The indictment does not give us a complete picture of the physical victims and material losses. The indictment makes do with a few general phrases about the period up to 20 November, but for those who suffered from the boycott and the sticks and stones that were used to support it, namely the Jews of Adzhival, things were not so easy. The words "beating Jews," with which the indictment is content to describe the attacks, convey very poorly the sequence of events and even more poorly the physical suffering of the victims. We can now supplement the indictment with a few scenes that Jewish witnesses described at trial.

Yankev Baritski related how hooligans entered his store, beat him, knocked out five of his teeth, threw down his wife and stomped on her, broke the store windows, and stole money. How did the court rule on this case at the beginning of June 1936? It sentenced four attackers to one year in jail and ten attackers to six months, but delayed the imposition of the penalty for three years so the hooligans were free to continue their "patriotic" work.

The pogrom in Pshitik was absolutely of the same style and character. Three Jews were killed, tens of Jews were seriously wounded, and many more were lightly wounded. Material damage was enormous. Here we will again quote the indictment even though it is clear to the most superficial reader that the prosecuting attorney, the author of the indictment, had a strong tendency to blame Jews for the pogrom, absolving the real pogromists and minimizing Jewish physical suffering and material damages. While it would certainly be worthwhile to quote this interesting and important document in its entirety, we lack the space to do so and must be content with substantial quotations:

> The town of Pshitik in the district of Radom has a population of 3,000, nearly 90 percent Jews. For a long time it was an arena of anti-Jewish excesses that took place especially on market days and were a result of the boycott agitation of the Endek party. These excesses were not limited to demands on the rural population who came to the market not to buy from Jews but involved threatening buyers, beating them, vandalizing Jewish stores, and breaking the windows of Jewish houses. These actions

sharpened especially since the events in Adzhival at the end of November 1935, when several peasants were killed by the police. Acts of terrorism also took place in the Pshitik region, about which exaggerated rumours would make their way to the town and increase nervousness among the Jewish as well as the Christian population. The fact that several Christian stores were opened in Pshitik contributed to the heightened tension in town.

After recording how the masses resisted the police, how the pogrom began, and how a shot killed Vyeshnyak, a Christian, the indictment sketches the following picture of the pogrom itself:

> The excesses began on Warsaw Street, not far from the bridge. At first the masses tore into the house of Rokhl Milshteyn. They tore off the shutters and broke the windows, through which they then entered the house. They knocked over the buffet and broke the table and wardrobes. Rokhl Milshteyn and Hersh Fish managed to hide themselves. On the same street, Aleksander Pitlevski beat Khaye Holtsman with a stick and Yuzef Tkatshik beat Moyshe Boymeyl with a stick that had wire wrapped around it. Only in the suburbs of Zakhenta and Podgayek did the pogrom intensify and take on a larger scale. Groups of 20–30 people armed with sticks broke into homes, demolishing tens of Jewish dwellings by tearing out their doors and windows with crowbars. In houses and stores, furniture and merchandise were destroyed or stolen....
>
> The most important incidents were the following: A group of attackers broke into the home of Sore Borenshteyn. One Pitlevskli beat Mrs Borenshteyn and others beat Gedalye Hempler. Yankev Borenshteyn, like his wife, was wounded with sticks and stones. Wardrobes, chairs and tables were destroyed. During the investigation forty-eight stones of various sizes were found in the house. In the home and store of Hinde Borenshteyn and in a second house the oven and beds were broken apart, featherbeds were ripped apart, and the windows knocked out. In the dwelling of Meyer-Leyb Taber, who was badly wounded, pitchforks, crowbars, stones, and sticks were found. There were blood markings on the walls. More than ten people broke into Mrs Pzhibishevitsh's store. They broke through three pairs of doors and in the last room they attacked Yisroel Pzhibishevitsh, breaking his left hand. Blood-stained sticks were later found on the bed in the kitchen. Windows were torn out of the home of Khaye Fridman, who was beaten with sticks. Mrs Fridman, who had given birth five weeks earlier, shielded her baby with her own body. The other children managed to run out of the house. The home of Alter Kozlovski was especially damaged. A group of 30 people broke the doors and windows, threw stones, and completely hacked apart the wardrobe in which Kozlovski and his children had hidden.

In the suburb of Podgayek about 15 homes were vandalized. In the business and home of Ber Taber all the furniture was broken and Taber himself was wounded five times in the head with a stone and is in serious condition. The walls were sprayed with blood. Blood markings were also found on the oven and even on the ceiling. Sixty stones were found in the house. Stones were also used to knock out the doors and windows of Feyge Shukh's home, where her eight children were hidden in the attic while she alone resisted the mass to prevent them from reaching the attic and so to save the children. Feyge Shukh was beaten with sticks. She suffered three head wounds, many wounds on her chest and shoulders, and damage to her spinal cord. Seventy-year-old Yokheved Palant ran out to the street during the excesses to find out the fate of her children. The mass surrounded her and beat her with sticks, seriously wounding her.

Aside from this, a series of houses were destroyed in the suburbs of Zakhenta and Podgayek. The most extreme expression of the wild actions took place in the house of the blacksmith, Rogulski, near which they laid Vyeshnyak's dead body. In that house, the mob broke into the apartment of the shoemaker, Yosef Minkovski. A stone thrown through the window hit fifteen-year-old Gavriel Minkovski, who was knocked unconscious. Minkovski's other three sons, between the ages of six and fourteen, hid under a bed. At the last moment Minkovski and his wife, Khaye, ran out to the front room, where they were attacked with sticks. There Minkovski was killed, and near him his wife fell from the blows visited on her. She died later in hospital.

They pulled six-year-old Shmuel Minkovski out from under the bed and beat his head with wooden sticks. Hersh and Eliyohu Minkovski were saved because they were hidden deep under the bed.

The autopsy on their parents showed that Yosef had five head wounds, three of them fatal. Khaye had three serious wounds, and in addition part of her brain was destroyed. Gavriel Minkovski was also seriously wounded. Six-year-old Shmuel suffered three head wounds. Due to psychological trauma, Gavriel was unable to provide a declaration.

Based on many witness reports, a series of attackers were implicated in the murder of the blacksmith, Minkovski, and the wounding of his son. Minkovski's body lay in a puddle of blood. Twenty stones, a broken stick, and a bloodied axe were found in the room. It seems that the death of the Minkovskis and the destruction of their home exhausted the hatred of the masses and sated their thirst for vengeance. The excesses slowly came to an end.

At approximately the same time in another corner of Pshitik, at the so-called "Pyaskes," young peasants attacked the Jew, Khaim Boymeyl, and wanted to throw him into the water. Afterwards, horse traders

Shloyme Teper and A. Berkovitsh were attacked with sticks and knives. Berkovitsh's nose was broken. Avrohom Goldberg suffered many serious head wounds and a broken left hand.

The Pshitik trial in Radom was ongoing during the writing of this work. During the two weeks of the trial to date it became clear that the fourteen Jewish accused, surrounded on all sides by wild, enraged masses, could at most be suspected of trying to defend themselves. The attempt of people to defend themselves and protect women and children, not to allow themselves to be slaughtered like sheep, responding with human dignity and honour to attacks and beatings, grabbing a piece of iron when someone raises a knife—such human reactions are the only bright moments in the entire trial. One shudders at the murderers, robbers, and assailants behaving with such audacity in court, without one iota of regret, so pleased with themselves, with a quiet but beaming threat to continue beating and murdering Jews with still more fervour and cruelty at the first opportunity. An emotionally stirring harmony and audacity pervades those who are on trial, their alibi witnesses, and their lawyer-friends. They all feel like heroes, like nationalist fighters, like first-rate patriots.

However, the trial in Radom also demonstrates that the indictment far from fully uncovered the whole truth. The physical and psychological wounds were many more and much deeper. One cannot even estimate material damages in broken windows, smashed-in doors, destroyed furniture, torn clothing and bedding, stolen merchandise, and ruined stalls. There is an even greater loss: a few weeks after the Pshitik pogrom, the antisemitic newspaper *Dziennik Narodowy* {*National Daily*}, Warsaw, 25 March 1936] related with joy that the town had lost several tens of Jewish market stalls and gained several tens of Christian market stalls; that in Adzhival, eight Polish market stalls and six Polish stores were opened; and in Dzhevitze, four Christian stores, and in Opotshne two new Christian butcher shops, opened, and in Konske three new Christian butcher shops. The joyous article ended thusly: "We do not have to add that Jews do not dare to show themselves in the surrounding villages. As practice shows, we can get by without Jews."

Even before the 1936 pogrom, the Endek newspaper, *Tygodnik Polityczny* {*Weekly Political*}, 16 February 1936, wrote: "After the latest events in Opotshne, the anti-Jewish atmosphere strengthened so much that Jews simply have no one to engage in trade with. According to material sent by Pshitik's Jews to the local administrator, the Endeks are terrorizing Jewish stores and market stalls. Whether this is true does not interest us. The fact is, 600 Jewish families in Pshitik now lack the means to earn a living and must choose between starving or emigration. It is very realistic to expect that very soon a pure Polish Pshitik will replace Jewish Pshitik."

However the trial in Radom ends, the victory of the Endeks is certain. Their goal becomes realistic more slowly than they would like, but Pshitik is on the way to becoming "purely Polish" because the mood of the Jewish population is more than despondent. Up to 150 families have already left Pshitik and whenever one speaks with a Jew from Pshitik, one hears the same thing: "In Pshitik things will not improve!"[16]

We now arrive at the pogrom in Minsk-Mazovyetsk, which took place from the evening of 1 June until 5 June, 1936. Minsk-Mazovyetsk is 37 km from Warsaw, an hour by train and three-quarters of an hour by car. Therefore, it is almost a suburb of Poland's capital.

From an antisemitic standpoint this was the ideal, most rewarding, most effective pogrom. More than 4,000 of Minsk-Mazovyetsk's 6,000 Jews fled the city! The panic was so great, the fear was already so deep in the soul and pervasive in the mind that more than two-thirds of the Jewish population abandoned their homes and all their worldly possessions. Even the old and the ill were left behind. And precisely in this pogrom nobody was killed, in contrast to the other pogroms. Of the more than fifty wounded, the majority were lightly wounded and only ten or twelve seriously wounded. The nineteen-year-old son of the wounded Jew, Gelbard, lost his mind from fear and is now in a Warsaw hospital, screaming "Save us! They're beating us!" Characteristically for the Minsk-Mazovyetsk pogrom, there was little robbery. There was more destruction and mayhem.

---

16 On 26 June 1936, the following verdict was delivered by the Radom court regarding the Jewish accused because they defended themselves in the Pshitik pogrom: Yekhiel Lesko was sentenced to eight years in jail, Eliezer Kirshentsvzayg to six years, Yisroel Fridman to five years, Eliezer Felberg and Yankev Harburger to ten months, Leybl Lenko and Moyshe Pertsh to six months. The forty-two Polish accused who were responsible for the pogrom received light sentences, from six months to one year in jail. The four Poles whom the judge blamed for the murder of the Minkovski couple were freed. This decision elicited a heated reaction in the Jewish population of Poland. On 30 June a protest strike took place among Jews in the entire country.

Fig. 5 People examining a house that was burned down in the 1936 Minsk-Mazovyetsk pogrom. ©Archives of the YIVO Institute for Jewish Research, New York, http://polishjews.yivoarchives.org/archive/index.php?p=digitallibrary/digitalcontent&id=2804

The locals characterized it as follows: the "party ideational pogromists" had been given an order not to cause great loss of life or engage in pillaging, thereby preserving the economic character and "ideational integrity" of the struggle. Throwing a stone to the head, striking the shoulders with a stick, breaking windows, doors, and furniture, tearing bedding and clothing, pouring gasoline on merchandise, and mixing sugar with salt—all these were counted as acts in the framework of the "economic" struggle, thus limiting the "spiritual" struggle. Only the joiners, the unorganized and undisciplined pogromists, and plain criminal elements stepped over the line, beating Jews bloody and crippling them, bringing home clothing and all manner of other merchandise.

This characterization contains much truth. The organizers of the pogrom, no matter how ready they were for murder and bloody attacks, aimed more at causing the Jewish population to run away by severing the economic roots that bound them to the city, tearing them away from their occupations for as long as possible, paralyzing their economic activity as much as possible, and strengthening the tendency and dream of emigration in the Jewish population. Indeed, for eight days

1. The pogroms in Poland, 1935–37

in succession, all Jewish businesses were locked and work ceased in all Jewish workshops. And it took another eight days until, bit by bit, the stores were reopened and work resumed.

It is understandable and also natural that the organizers of the pogrom were in a hurry to reap with delight what they had sown with joy. In fact, the entire antisemitic press initiated a huge campaign promoting the idea that Poles should exploit the auspicious moment to grab Jewish jobs. On 8 June 1936, *Dziennik Narodowy* wrote thusly:

> Last Wednesday, 3 June, a market took place in Minsk-Mazovyetsk. This time it was free of Jews. A large volume of business took place in the Polish stalls and Polish stores. Large new vistas opened up for Polish trade and craft work in Minsk-Mazovyetsk. They must be exploited! We must take trade and craft work in our own hands!
>
> What is lacking and what we must undertake can be inferred from provided statistics. There is room for stores selling food, linen, men's accessories, clothing, meat, agricultural tools, and meat. We need tailors, shoemakers, hat makers, and saddlers. Trade at market stalls has exceptional potential for development.

On the first market day after the pogrom, the Endek party distributed thousands of copies of a legal call to arms. Here are its contents:

> Polish merchants and craft workers! Most Polish craft work and trade remains in the hands of Jews! Polish workshops are going under—under the force of taxes, destitution, and Jewish competition!
>
> Jewish benevolent society funds and professional organizations hand out millions {of *zloty*} to destroy the growth of Christian jobs.
>
> Let us create Christian organizations that will be able to repel this assault!
>
> The peasant and the worker require Polish stores, Polish market stalls, and Polish craft work.
>
> Anti-Jewish Poland will minimally triple the income of Polish workshops and create thousands of new Christian jobs.
>
> Establish Polish workshops where the *kapote*[17] class long dominated, bring into the workshops material that until now was produced mainly by Jews.
>
> Organize yourselves in the ranks of the Polish nation! Our slogan is the unity of Poles!

Apart from this legal call to arms there was another illegal one which

---

17 {A *kapote* is a long black coat traditionally worn by devout Jews.}

no longer speaks an "economic language." The illegal call to arms reads as follows:

> The Jewish commune has obscenely murdered quartermaster Boyak. Jewish bullets felled Vatslavski, Grotkovski, and Vyeshnyak. In Lemberg blood flowed. There the Jew demonstrated and shouted: "Down with the army, down with the Church!" Hatred toward the army was confirmed by a shot against those who fought for Poland's freedom. Poles, you have sworn by Boyak's coffin to fight until the Jewish "blizzard" turns to dust. The spilled blood of soldiers and the majesty of the army, which is the holiness of Poland, demand vengeance from you. Peasants, workers, and intellectuals! In one row in struggle against the Jewish community. For violence we pay with violence, for the blood of soldiers, the blood of Jews! Death to the Jews!

The quoted documents (many more of which could be presented because tens of newspapers write thusly every day and illegal calls to arms often have more murderous contents), testify to the close connection between the struggle against Communism and extending one's hand to seize the market booth beside which the poor Jew stands. Here, the patriotic world to come is held to be compromised by the market of this world.

It should also be noted here that in Minsk-Mazovyetsk there were many cases of Christians not just hiding their Jewish neighbours but also defending them and risking their lives for them. There were also plenty of cases that demonstrate that the hate psychosis is contagious, but we are used to this. Cases demonstrating that there are still people who get excited about every wild attack on Jews make a bigger impression.

A permanent pogrom

The permanent pogrom plague that has befallen Polish Jewry expresses itself in its clearest form in the list of cities where attacks, excesses, explosive bombs, stink bombs, beatings, and wounds by stabbing and strikes on the shoulders with wooden sticks and iron rods were witnessed. Before me lies a list of more than 150 cities and towns where attacks occurred. Many of them have been immersed for a whole year in a firestorm of beatings and breaking windows, stabbings, and throwing bombs. Here we see the *ethnic* character of the Polish pogrom wave. Organized by a legal mass party, the permanent pogrom is supported by active and passive sympathizers from the broadest circle of all Polish classes. It paralyzes the Jewish masses, creates panic in the Jewish population, disorganizes Jewish society, forcibly tears livelihoods from Jewish hands, shifting the full attention of the Jewish individual and the Jewish community to fleeing, emigrating, saving oneself. In this way it weakens the courage to struggle for the jobs that have been saved. All this cries out from the tens and hundreds of attacks and murders that have spread like a plague and continue for months and years.

From a list covering the period May 1935 to August 1936, one sees that the pogrom wave grew from month to month both in its geographical spread and its intensity as measured by the number of wounded in each place.

The list includes the names of 762 wounded individuals, most seriously wounded, whose names are listed because they required medical attention and therefore registered themselves. We count 1,289 wounded and beaten individuals in all. This number excludes the "few" and the "many" casualties mentioned in tens of places. It is difficult to know how many people with wounds and holes in their skull are described by these vague terms.

The Polish censor is highly capricious, so there were months when newspapers were not allowed to publish any news about attacks and excesses. Thus, in Warsaw there was a period when the Jewish press could not disclose any information on attacks in the province. We found out about the victims in Adzhival and many other places only at trial, half a year after they occurred. We must therefore assume that the data about the number of wounded and beaten, even according to the list of the cities and towns, is far from the actual number. The actual number of beaten and wounded certainly approaches 3,000.

From the list we also learn that 112 bombs were thrown in the space of sixteen months. This is a topic that needs to be handled separately; it is a completely new method in the antisemitic struggle, an innovation on the part of Polish hooligans. The Endek party organized special units for throwing bombs at Jewish businesses. It goes without saying that when the bombs explode, they do not distinguish between merchandise and people. And enough people have died because of these bombs, although the "ideational patriots" make an effort to lay the bombs at night, thereby underlining that they do not intend to harm Jews as much as the Jewish store, knowing full well that with the collapse of the store the Jew would also be destroyed. At a trial of twenty-seven bomb throwers in Lodz, it emerged that every member of the assault group vowed as follows: "I swear before God to execute every order, to keep each instruction secret, and never to betray the vanguard of the Endek party, so help me God!"

Bombs were thrown, people were killed, and businesses were ruined in tens of cities. And until today the party whose members throw the bombs remains legal and can agitate openly for eradicating Jews and driving them away. Unfortunately, we cannot deal extensively with individual cases here.

Arson, too, is a special Polish method of antisemitic struggle. Of course, we have discussed only cases in which it is absolutely clear that the fire was the work of Endek bandits.

Unfortunately, we must also refrain from discussing in detail terror against Jewish students in higher education, which has become a "holy tradition" every autumn. This year it assumed an especially cruel character and stretched over the entire winter, from November 1935 until the end of April 1936. No fewer than 100 Jewish male and female students were wounded last winter. Among them were about ten who will remain cripples for the rest of their lives. Not long ago, Rozenman, a Jewish student, was wounded by an Endek student in Lemberg. After suffering in bed for several weeks, he died in June.

The dry numbers derived from the list of the wounded in cities where there were attacks and excesses do not convey even in the palest form and by the weakest measure the truly tragic situation that is signified by the term "permanent pogrom." One must remember in this connection that Polish Jewry lacks an institution that specializes in collecting material about the pogroms, attacks, excesses, bombs, cases of arson, student acts of terror, and plain hooliganistic assaults with knives and sticks. We therefore believe it would be useful to provide the chronicle of such events over two days, 25 and 26 June 1936, based on material in Jewish newspapers. This chronicle will allow the reader to be transported into the infested and poisoned atmosphere in which Polish Jewry happens to live.

On 25 June 1936, the Warsaw newspaper *Haynt* brought the following news:

- A delegation of Jews from Volye, where a bomb was recently planted under a Jewish business, turned to Senator Professor Shor and explained the terrible situation that had arisen there.
- On the night of Wednesday, 24 June, hooligans attacked Jews in various places and wounded ten men. When these incidents were reported to the police, nobody intervened.
- Last night in Old-Milosne hooligans set fire to the bakery and the stable of Benyomen Breytshteyn. The buildings were completely burned down. Two weeks earlier a bomb was placed under the bakery. It caused enormous damage and injured Yisroel Loyfer and his wife. They remain in a Warsaw hospital until today.

In the same issue, a special correspondent reported on an attack in the town of Mishlenitse:

In a row of businesses the windows were smashed, the doors broken, the shutters destroyed. Broken porcelain dishes and spilled grain, peas, and flour were on the floors. Everything was mixed in a pile from which an unbearable stench exuded. The attackers drenched the merchandise with gasoline, oil, and vinegar so that it could not be sold.

The first to suffer from the band were the Jews, Yosef Emer and Hersh Vestraykh. They were loading merchandise on a wagon, preparing to take it to market. The band beat them badly and set the wagon and the merchandise on fire. The assailants did not depart after that but waited until everything was consumed by flames. The baker, Yehude-Leyb Vaksnberg was also severely beaten, resulting in serious head wounds. The hooligans broke the shutters and entered Reyzl Goldshteyn's colonial food goods and porcelain store. They then demolished the store and its contents. Next they broke into the tailor shop of Yeshue Blumenshtok. There they poured acidic liquids on many suits and other clothes such as coats, furs, and so on. They piled these things together in two places, in the store and in the market square, and set them on fire. Just then the baker, Yakubovski, drove up with a wagon of bread. The hooligans drove away Yakubovski with blows and told the Christian wagon driver to divide the bread among the hungry Poles free of charge.

The *Folkstsaytung* of 26 June 1936 announced:

We received a report from Minsk-Mazovyetsk that Wednesday night several non-civilians {police officers} attacked three Jews in the street and then shot after them: Khaim Matushevski, Yisroel Rozenberg, and Dovid Morgenshtern. Later they beat Yosef Vaserman. The same night, an attempt was made to set fire to a Jewish house on Shenitser Street. Luckily, the perpetrators were noticed and driven off, leaving behind a rag soaked in gasoline and a package of matches.

The *Haynt* of 26 June announced:

Fogelnest, the Chair of the Minsk-Mazovyetsk aid society, delivered a report to the Warsaw committee: 417 people received urgent help, 45 families received help with reconstruction, 1,300 new windows were installed with the help of the committee, 60 gates were repaired, and 350 families are waiting for reconstruction help.

In the same issue of *Haynt*:

In Warsaw over the last two days there arrived delegations from a whole series of cities and towns, including Tshenstokhov, Garvolin, Novidvor {Nowy Dwór}, as well as many cities in Volin, where the magistrates had begun an extermination campaign against Jewish merchants standing in markets with tables and booths, ordering them to clear out. They allegedly wanted to implement new arrangements, but in reality they want to remove Jewish merchants and give their places to Christians.

The *Folkstsaytung* of 26 June announced:

Yesterday, some Jews were sitting on a bench and talking in Krashinski {Krasiński} Garden (Nalevki Street, Warsaw). Police officer 1659 approached them and started shouting "To Palestine! If not, then to Minsk-Mazovyetsk!" He then took a rubber billy club and delivered blows to their shoulders.

In the same issue:

The Jewish woman, Roze Kon, was murdered tonight in the eastern Galicia village of Tsigane, Bartshev county. She had lived in the village for many years and had a little grocery store. She lived with her mother and her nine-year-old daughter. Recently the Endeks blocked customers' entry to her store. In the end they murdered her. The police arrested a certain Endek who had the previous week kept watch on the store and prevented Christian customers from entering it.

In the same day's issue of *Moment*:

Yesterday at about 9 pm in Warsaw's Saxon Garden antisemitic attacks recurred. On a path by the water several Jews were sitting on a bench, when suddenly a band of Christian students wearing academic caps tried to throw the bench and the Jews in the water. The cries of the Jews attracted a crowd of Christians who casually observed the "spectacle," giving courage to the students. In the turmoil Jews started running away. One Christian entered a candy shop and called the police. Soon a police detachment arrived and dispersed the hooligans without arresting any of them. While running away they bloodied the Jew, Henrik Levkovitsh.

The two-day chronicle will suffice. The reader should not think that these days were exceptional. Polish Jews experienced many tens if not hundreds of such eventful pogrom days this year. This is the atmosphere in which they live. This is the air they breathe.

The normality of fear

Living in fear, constantly feeling uncertain, apprehensive that in time someone will stab you with a knife or smash your head or your legs with a stick—this is the "normal" situation in which Polish Jewry has found itself for nearly three years. For years, Jews have been going around with tension in their shoulders. And not only the Jew who travels with his pack of merchandise from the small town to the countryside; not only the Jew who crosses the border of his small-town ghetto; not only the Jew from the mid-size city who ends up on some out-of-the-way Christian street; but also the Jew from the liveliest streets of Warsaw while he visits the largest public garden in the centre of the capital—he, too, carries in his shoulders the unease and the fear. The same is true of the liveliest streets in Lodz, Bialystok, Vilna, Lemberg, Krakow, Grodno, Brisk, and tens of other large and middle-size cities in independent Poland, cities with hundreds of thousands of residents, with a Jewish population comprising at a minimum one-third and often one-half of the city population. Thousands of Jews have been wounded over the last three years in these "cultural" centres of revived independent Poland, wounded by a piece of iron to the head, by a knife to the chest, by a stone to the eye, by a club to the back. It is therefore not surprising that the shoulders of Polish Jews are so tense that, hearing the slightest stir, the tiniest sudden movement behind them, causes them to look around or try to disappear as quickly as possible.

Wounded people number as many as 10,000 over the last two-and-a-half years. They are victims of the permanent pogrom that persists for years and poisons every day, every hour. You traverse lively streets.

People run and push, hurrying home or to the store. The world is busy with its normal worries and sorrows. And suddenly a Jew falls, be he elderly or young, fainting with a bloody wound in his chest or his head. The organs of power soon restore order. This means that they soon send the Jew to a hospital while in the streets the everyday pace of life resumes, just as if nothing happened. Very rarely, the knife wielder or the hero with the club is caught and is taken to the police station.

One can confidently claim that for the last two-and-a-half years there was not one day when no Jews were wounded in Warsaw or Lodz. The severely wounded, who arrive for help, are known; the lightly wounded are ashamed to speak up, so they take a carriage home or to the doctor and nobody knows anything about a Jew being hit on the back with a stick or on the head with a stone. However, thousands of Jews know that they have experienced a hooligan's stick or knife; tens or perhaps hundreds of thousands feel that their backs are fair game, that their heads may at any moment be hit by a stone or pierced by a knife. Fear is transmitted to millions, and so *a psychology of constant unease and uncertainty is created*, a constant nervousness.

We are certain that any other people, finding itself in similar circumstances, abandoned to the hooligans, unarmed and defenceless, would become the victim of much more intense fear and nervousness. "Don't judge your friend until you are in his place"[18] is what we would say to all those who have the gall to deride Jewish fear....

Let us deal with facts. On 24 August 1937, a Jew, L. Koze, was on the way from Tshenstokhov to the Zaremba-Koshtshelna market. On the way he was stopped by a group from the National-Radical party, whose youth leader is Colonel Koc.[19] The national heroes cut out the Jew's eyes. They took nothing from the old, weak Jew in order to demonstrate that this was not a robbery but a "national struggle." These are indeed knights!

On 29 August 1937 a Jewish lawyer by the name of Yosef Nartenberg was walking on the streets of Drohobitsh {Drohobycz}, a city with more than 30,000 inhabitants, 12,000 of them Jews. Suddenly someone stabbed him in the back, leaving the knife in him. Doctors removed the knife and determined that Nartenberg's condition was serious. The incident

---

18 {*Pirkei avot* (*Ethics of the Fathers*) 2:4.}

19 {Sanacja politician Adam Koc announced the formation of the *Obóz Zjednoczenia Narodowego* (OZN; Camp of National Unity) in February 1937 and became its leader. OZN won Poland's 1938 legislative election.}

occurred during the day but the attacker was not apprehended.

Here is another hero from the Polish nationalist camp: in Uyazd {Ujazd} in the district of Lodz, a Jew, Yekhiel Yakubovitsh, passed by a building where several labourers were working. One Bogutshak, a member of the Endek party, flung a shovel full of lime in his face. The Jew's screams attracted people who started washing his eyes with water. The lime started to burn. He was brought straight to Warsaw for an operation but was permanently blinded. Yekhiel-Meir Yakubovitsh has a wife and children and is just forty-two years old. He was blinded in July 1937. The national hero was sentenced to a year in jail. By comparison, for possessing a booklet from Soviet Russia one is sentenced to seven, eight, and often ten years of hard prison.

On 7 October 1936, B. Zilbershteyn, a bootmaker from Parisov {Parysów}, took a bus from Shedlits {Siedlce} to Stotsk. Because the bus does not go as far as Parisov, he disembarked in order to walk home, a distance of 16 km. In the village of Gast {Gózd?}, gentiles attacked him, throwing stones. The stones hit his left eye. Bloodied with a head wound, he barely managed to drag himself to the home of the local landowner, where he received first aid. After weeks in bed he was brought to Warsaw, where his left eye was removed. His right eye, which was also in great danger, was saved. The names of the hooligans were determined so they could be brought to trial but meanwhile they remained free. It was determined that these were not just demoralized or dissolute gentile boys who were entertaining themselves at the expense of a poor Jew. They were representatives of the younger generation of the new, free Poland that lays claim to power in the country.

A Jewish water carrier, Henekh Lipshits, was walking on the streets of Radom. A hooligan attacked him, poked out his eye, but was not apprehended. This occurred on 7 May 1937 in a city with 80,000 inhabitants. Nationalist, free Poland also carries on a struggle with the Jewish water carrier, the poorest of the poor, the weakest of the weak.

The following fact shows how much the wild animal can be awoken in a person: in Zamoshtsh {Zamość}, a Polish architect by the name of Dombrovski was arrested for illegal work for the extreme right. On the way to detention he comes across a Jew with a beard, Yankev Fraynt. Love for his fatherland burns in the Polish architect's heart, so he runs over to the Jew, grabs him by the beard, drags him along for quite a distance, then rips out part of his beard. The representative of state authority who was taking Dombrovski, the political criminal, to detention does not consider it necessary to hinder the "national fighter" in his patriotic work. In September 1937, the representative of state authority knows full well that the arrested architect is a member of a party that is conducting negotiations about entering the government, and one does not argue with an arrestee who stands at the threshold of power.

Let us now see whether the situation is better in big cities such as Lodz, with its more than 600,000 residents, 200,000 of them Jews.

On 25 May 1937 a Jewish woman, Khane Mogolnitzke, and her six-year-old daughter were walking on Zgerzhe Street in Lodz. A person from the national camp pushed them in front of a truck and both fell under its wheels. Luckily, the driver managed to stop. The mother was completely bloodied and she was taken to the hospital. The child was fine. But the incident shows the extent of the nationalist insanity.

The daily Lodz chronicle describes the "normal" attacks to which Jews have become accustomed—along with the accompanying anxiety.

On 2 November 1937, not far from the Baluty market, thirty-five-year-old Yosef Feld was walking in the street. It was daytime and foot traffic was heavy. Suddenly, Feld was stabbed. He was taken to the hospital in a hopeless situation. The assailants disappeared. Why was this Jew assaulted and not someone else? It was purely a matter of bad luck. None of the Jews who were then in the street had any connection to the attackers.

The Endeks hold a meeting in a hall in the centre of Lodz and Jews receive "gifts" afterwards. Here are the results of one evening on 7 October 1936: a girl, Beyle Sheynberg, suffered a haemorrhage from her wounds; a student, Yakub Fridman, suffered several head wounds; the boot maker, Refoel Rozenberg, was wounded multiple times on his face. All received first aid. The windows of many Jewish homes were broken.

Cases like the following occur almost daily: Khaim Arenshteyn and his daughter Leye were walking in a suburb of Lodz on 6 June 1936. Assailants broke the skull of the elderly Arenshtayn and severely wounded his daughter. On 12 January 1937 Borekh Shlagman was standing at 25 Pomorske Street with an apple cart. Two Christians approach him and tell him to give them a kilo of apples. They take the apples and start walking away. When the Jew asks for payment he is stabbed in his chest and his side. The assailants are not caught. The Jew is taken to the hospital. Such incidents occur often. A Jewish invalid, Gershn Yoskovitsh, whose blood had been spilled in the struggle for Polish independence, was approached by several riled up, nationalist lads. They poked out his eye, stabbed him, and overturned his booth of merchandise. Three of the assailants were arrested. On 8 October 1936, thirty-two-year-old Yekhiel Shtern—also an invalid from the Polish-Russian war in which he lost an eye—was attacked. His good eye was poked out, not on the external but on the internal battlefield, when he was assaulted by Polish nationalists.

Did any of these Jews have anything to do with their assailants before they were attacked? Absolutely not. They were all victims of chance. Here is an example. The Savitzki family, including several children, lived in the little town of Vlashtsheve, Kelts province. They had a small store. They had to flee because their windows were broken, they were beaten, and their lives were threatened. They fled to Lodz but their destiny followed them. Jewish destiny is similar to its bearers, to Jews themselves: it is stubborn. On 2 February 1937, when the father, Fayvl Savitzki, was walking with his son, Kopl, on Magistratske {Magistracka} Street, three hooligans attacked them. They stabbed young Kopl in the back and he fell immediately in a puddle of blood. The father started begging for mercy but he was kicked in the stomach and fell. The Polish patriots left nonchalantly. A few minutes passed before people came and took them to a hospital where they received first aid. Young Kopl remained there for months. Such is Jewish luck, Jewish destiny. It is impossible to escape it.

In a way, it is superfluous to write about Warsaw. Multiply the murders and attacks in Lodz by two or three and you have Warsaw. The Polish nationalist hooligans in Warsaw repeat the horrific actions seen in Lodz. Yet they also innovate. It is therefore worthwhile examining their innovations separately.

The third of May is a national holiday in Poland. Before the war it was a day of struggle against the tsarist regime and also a day of brotherhood among all the suffering and oppressed in tsarist Russia without regard for their ethnicity or religion. However, in independent Poland it became a pogrom day, a hellish day for the Jewish population. The same thing happens every year. The nationalist youth hold demonstrations during which they beat Jews, break the windows of Jewish businesses, throw stones at Jewish heads, and fill the streets with shouts of "Down with the Jews! Jews out of here!"

On 3 May 1937 the pogrom heroes remained true to the tradition. It is difficult to determine how many Jewish heads were hit by stones and how many Jewish backs were struck by nationalist sticks in honour of this holiday. What was new this year was that they caught two Jews on the bridge, Kalmen Lipshitz and Lozer Goldman, and threw them into the Vistula. It is difficult to convey in words this nationalist scene, the way in which the pogrom heroes of independent Poland dragged two Jews by their hands and feet and flung them from a high bridge deep into the same Vistula where just three decades ago Jewish revolutionaries used to drive out in small boats to hold illegal deliberations on how to free Poland from the Russian regime. Luckily also in 1937, in the Poland of pogroms and semi-fascism, workers rescued the honour of their fatherland. During the wild scene when Jews were thrown into the Vistula, several Polish workers who were passing by jumped into the water, saved the Jews, and thereby also the honour of the independent fatherland.

Another unique characteristic of the Warsaw hooligans is their attacks on, or throwing stones at, Jewish funerals. In the last two years this occurred around thirty times. Some ended with the living envying the dead. On 21 May 1936 the Jewish coachman, Berl Boshkovski, was severely wounded in the head during the funeral of Avrom Naftal and remained ill for the rest of his life. The coachman, Yankl Nyevyadomsky, who lost an eye after being struck by a stone, is also not among the lucky ones who are happy to be alive.

Yet another peculiarity: in the two Warsaw city parks—Saxon Garden in the city centre and Traugutt Park near the Jewish quarter—the beating of Jews does not cease. In broad daylight, when sick old men, women, mothers with young children in carriages, and people wanting to enjoy a little fresh air are sitting on benches, about ten young urchins suddenly turn up and start beating and chasing Jews with stones, clubs, and sticks. They throw themselves on the defenceless Jews and spare no one. Mothers scream, carriages with small children in them are toppled, old people run and shriek, and in the confusion a Christian is sometimes hit with a stick. By the time the police arrive there is no longer any trace of the hooligans.

In the evening the picture changes a little. They catch Jews and throw them in the Saxon Garden pond, stab them, and tear off their clothes. Jews refrain from going to the parks for a few days, but on a summer evening can people remain in their stifling, poor dwellings? They gather their courage and return to the park. For three years, hooligans, often wearing student hats, do their "national" work and the authorities "can't manage" to subdue their "heroes." The pogrom at the Saxon Garden in September 1937 persisted for entire weeks and wounded a few hundred Jews, about fifty so seriously that they will remain cripples, but also wounded about fifty hooligans, a few of them seriously. This admirable resistance of Jewish workers convinced the authorities to bring the pogrom to an end in one day. They were simply afraid of a civil war, the danger of which was in the air. It is therefore evident that the authorities know full well that in contemporary Poland there exists not only ethnic but also *social* gunpowder, and that every civil war, no matter how loaded with antisemitic gunpowder, can quickly spread and infect other groups and classes, with unexpected results.

On trains and ships

A separate section must be devoted to pogrom actions on the trains. There are certain lines where attacks and murders persist for months. For example, 50–60,000 Jews live along the Warsaw-Otvotsk {Otwock} line {just over 25 km}, many of whom travel to Warsaw daily because they are tied to the city by their business. The train is always packed with Jews. But ten or so hooligans armed with sticks, knives, clubs, stones, or pieces of iron are enough to terrorize hundreds of Jews on the train. After all, about twenty Jews sit in each car, some of whom are old, women, or weak people. At a station where the train stops for half a minute, ten hooligans jump in and as soon as the train starts moving they begin their patriotic work: beating, spitting in faces, tearing beards, and throwing out of the window hats and packages of merchandise that Jews are bringing from the city. And before the train stops at the next station, the hooligans jump off. It often transpires that, as the train travels down the tracks, one hears heart-breaking cries from the cars where they are tormenting old and defenceless people, but the conductors are never in the cars where the pogroms take place.

One cannot say that the authorities always permit beatings in the cars. As in many other cases, the authorities tolerate pogrom anarchy only to a certain extent. When the attacks become too bloody or too murderous, threatening to grow into a general brawl because the Jews begin to resist, the authorities impose order. A pause ensues. The pogromists move their work to another line or they relax for a few weeks, then repeat the story.

Here is a small picture of a twenty-minute trip of a Jew from Warsaw to Rembartov {Rembertów}. On 8 September 1937 a Jew, Yosef Vorhalter, entered a train compartment. Five Polish students sat in the compartment with him. As soon as the train started moving they threw themselves on the Jew and started beating him, choking him, and stomping on him with their feet. Several passengers from the neighbouring compartment responded to his cries—Christians who took pride in the actions of the young Polish generation. The Jew, bloodied and bruised, barely managed to exit the compartment and get himself home. One must understand that, in general, Jews enter a compartment only if the others seated in it are all Jews. However, Vorhalter boarded the train at the last minute before departure.

It has reached the point that on the Bendin {Będzin} line they began establishing ghetto cars for Jews. Conductors directed Jewish passengers to separate cars as they were about to enter the train. Understandably, the Jews protested. The authorities replied that their safety could not be guaranteed if they refused. Only after a meeting with the central authority were ghetto cars done away with. In practice, however, the ghetto exists and grows. The writer of these lines observed on tens of occasions how Jewish passengers look for compartments or cars where there are many Jews.

Citing examples of Jews bloodied in trains would mean listing hundreds of names, so we will mention only a few examples. Khaim Pomerants, a Jewish merchant, was travelling from Pyastov {Piastów} to Warsaw. A couple of hooligans entered his car not far from Warsaw and started bothering the Jew. He remained silent. Finally they grabbed the Jew, dragged him to the door, and threw him out of the train. A Christian woman who was nearby screamed and the train stopped. The Jew was found with broken arms and legs in a puddle of blood. The hooligans were not apprehended. In the chaos while the train had stopped they managed to disappear. One can say with certainty that if someone had said a good word about Soviet Russia in the car, he would not have managed to escape.

Here is another case that is characteristic in Poland today. The Jewish director of a factory was travelling in a second class car from Warsaw to Vilna. An intelligent-looking Christian, unable to find room in his compartment, told him to leave because a Pole cannot stand when a Jew sits. The Jew refused to answer. A few minutes later the Jew stood up and went to the door. The Christian followed him and tried to throw him off the moving train. However, the Jew was a healthy man. He threw the Christian down, took a revolver out of his pocket, and declared that he will shoot anyone who comes close to him. The Christian sat on the ground until the next station. The police determined that the Christian is a high school teacher. Such are those bringing up the young Polish generation.

On ships, too, tens of cases of Jews being beaten have taken place. For instance, on the boat from Warsaw to Vlotslavek {Włocławek}, there were several cases of Jews being beaten last summer. Much has been written about the case of the Jewish historian, Shimen Dubnov, but it is worth memorializing the story for the coming generations.

Professor Dubnov was in Vilna for the congress of the Jewish Scientific Institute {YIVO} in August 1936. He and his daughter and grandson went for an excursion on the Viliye {Vilija; the river that passes through Vilna}. "Poznantshiks"[20] were on the boat. They threw themselves on the grandson, who was about twenty years old, and they wanted to throw him in the river. One can imagine the situation of the mother and the seventy-five-year-old grandfather. The captain piloted the boat to the uninhabited, forested shoreline, where he dropped off the three Jews because he could otherwise not guarantee the safety of the young man.

Let us end this section with a case that is a bit comical but clearly reflects the rightless condition of the Jewish population and the travesty of the relationship that state organs have with Jews. The case was publicized on 20 November 1937 in the Polish workers' newspaper, *Robotnik*, an organ of the Polish Socialist Party. Khaim Fridman was traveling by train from Sosnovits {Sosnowiec} to Katovits {Katowice}

---

20 {Germanized soldiers from the Polish military divisions in Posen who had a well-earned reputation for being brutally antisemitic.}

when a hooligan bloodied him with a knife. In Katovits at the train station Fridman had to pay a one *zloty* fine for smearing the bench he was sitting on with blood. The editor adds that the number of the receipt from bloc number 5833 may be found in the editorial office.

Child pogroms

Sodom? Barbarism? Official mockery of more than three million people? All three expressions are too weak to characterize the situation. But we are still only at the beginning. The related facts are not even the most terrifying in Poland today. We will conclude this work with the child pogroms in which Polish children beat Jewish children. Both sides of this black coin are terrible. And there is another question: Whose condition is more deplorable, that of the Jewish victims or the Polish assailants?

We will have to exhaustively discuss elsewhere the Polish pogrom epic in higher education, which has already dragged on for five or six years. Here we discuss actual schoolchildren in public primary schools. Only then will it become clear that, in tens of public primary schools, Polish children are beating their Jewish classmates with whom they sit on the same bench; that in tens of public primary and high schools, Polish students demand separate benches for Jewish students; that, leaving school, Jewish children run away quickly because they are afraid to remain standing with the Polish children; that there are already tens of cases in which Jewish children stop going to school for fear of the Polish student majority—only then does it become clear how far demoralization has dropped. Even in Germany there has not been a single case in which children demanded separate benches for their Jewish colleagues, and even in the Hitler atmosphere there are only very seldom cases of children taking a stand against their Jewish classmates. That children can be more pitiless and wilder than grown-ups is well known. The facts brilliantly illustrate this fact.

In the centre of the Jewish quarter in Warsaw there are a few evening schools for youth. These schools became a tragedy for the Jewish residents of the quarter. Number 2 Nalevki Street, Simons' Passage {Pasaż Simonsa}, and 60 Dluge {Długa} Street are the addresses of the schools and therefore the nests of the serious hooligans. When students exit the schools they start beating Jewish fellow students or Jews in general. Every evening when the students leave school, in the area from Nalevki to Theatre Square, attacks take place that often end with several Jews driven to the hospital. We have before our eyes a list of names of tens of Jews who were severely wounded by these student hooligans. These completion courses for student apprentice artisans, opened in the centre of the Jewish quarter where Jews comprise 90% or more of all artisans, now have almost no Jewish students because Jewish youth are simply afraid. In the courses where a few Jewish students remain, the instructors let the Jewish students out ten minutes early so they can have time to save themselves from their hooligan colleagues.

In recent years several Jewish organizations created suburban half-day "colonies" in which children from the poorest Jewish streets could have the possibility of breathing fresh air for a few hours each day in the summer months. In Warsaw more than 40,000 Jewish children used these colonies. However, during the last couple of summers a ridiculously small number of children took advantage of them because their mothers were afraid to leave their children in the suburbs. The mothers' fear does not derive from exaggerated fantasies. The children were showered with stones, hundreds of the children were attacked and beaten, returning from the fresh air with head wounds. Some of these half-day colonies were guarded by the police all summer.

It is now an unwritten rule that Jews should not send their children to colonies set up by municipal institutions or state insurance companies that are intended for the general population. In the summer of 1936 there were still a few Jews who did so, but they received such a lesson that they will never again dare to take such a risk. Their children returned home with tears and wounds, cursing the day they risked going to a colony with a majority of Polish children.

A few facts will show us how far the chaos can reach. Jewish children were travelling on a streetcar to a half-day colony near Povonzek, a Warsaw suburb. Three times the streetcar was pelted with rocks and twice the children and their caregivers were beaten. In 1936, in Holenuvek {Helenów}, not far from Warsaw, a colony was sponsored by the department of social insurance. Two hundred children attended, thirty of them Jews. To get rid of these thirty children, a choir was created where the children were taught antisemitic songs. That did not work because the Jewish children were from the poorest Jewish classes, without fresh air at home and hungry for a little soup and the open sky. They gritted their teeth and remained under the sun which they see so seldom in the cellars and poor dwellings where they lived with their parents. Then the children and their teachers adopted more effective means. They started beating the Jews. At first there were just a few attacks far from the colony's building. Then, group attacks took place on individual Jewish students. Later, they attacked entire groups of Jewish students. The Jewish students had to leave.

And it was not only boys who attacked other boys. Nine- and ten-year-old girls attacked their Jewish female classmates from class and beat them. A notice in a Warsaw Jewish newspaper on 16 December 1936 read: "Nine-year-old Jewish students Tselinka Shapiro and Manya Beker were on the way from the public school on Spokoyne {Spokojna} Street when they were attacked by older female students who beat them until they fainted. Passers-by picked them up and brought them home."

We have to this point spoken of attacks by schoolchildren on schoolchildren. One must add that youth play no small part in adult attacks on Jews, and the adult hooligans themselves do not spare Jewish children. For example, in Warsaw's Krashinski Garden on 27 October 1937 a carriage in which the child of the Jewish office worker, Dovid Meganek, lay was doused with gasoline. The friend of the person who spilled the gasoline threw a lit match into the carriage. The child's coat caught fire. They barely managed to smother the flames and save the child, who was taken to an infirmary for treatment.

It is no better in the provinces and often worse. Here is a communication from the town of Kartshev {Karczew} stating that Jewish parents have stopped sending their children to school because Christian children beat up the Jewish children. They complain to the teachers, who laugh and joke that they can get along without Jewish students. In Vilna the most active participants in all antisemitic scuffles are not only students from the high schools but also students from the primary schools. They break windows in Jewish homes and businesses, and take part in riots on Jewish-populated streets and pickets boycotting Jewish stores. Not infrequently Jews are also beaten in the schools. At the end of 1936, thirty-five Polish students were handed over to the district attorney's office for breaking windows. In Pshitik, Polish children on an excursion knocked out two teeth of Goldshteyn, a Jewish student.

1. The pogroms in Poland, 1935–37

The teachers watched the scene cold-bloodedly and joked: "Not so bad, he's still alive, the little Jew-boy." But not all teachers are infected with hatred, and we can offer a few examples.

There is a seminary for Christian teachers in the town of Shenitse {Siennica}, near Minsk-Mazovyetsk. Three seminary students met a Jewish boy, Goldshteyn, on the street and beat and bloodied him. The boy's mother complained to the director of the seminary. In the middle of a class, the three hooligans were not just thrown out of the class but expelled from the seminary. At the request of their parents and also perhaps for fear of revenge, Goldshteyn's mother went to the director and declared that she forgave the assailants.

Lodz, too, can take pride in its Polish students, who are in the first row of all the demonstrations of extreme antisemites in the city and also the first to beat and torment Jews. They are the distributors of poisonous literature; they are the most active picketers at the market; nor do they spare children and old people. A Jew of more than seventy years, Yekhiel Koyfman, took a train from Warsaw to Lodz. Near Lodz a group of students became interested in the old man's white beard. It ended with the students setting his beard on fire. Luckily, several nearby Christians saved the old man and also drove the students away. During school excursions there have been tens of attacks on Jewish students by Christian students. It reached a point that Jewish students had to be escorted by the police when they went on excursions.

We can end this chapter with a case that illustrates both the general situation of Jewish children in Polish schools and the recourse to which they must unfortunately resort in order to save themselves from physical torment.

On Novogrodske Street in Warsaw there is a horticultural school. Among a few hundred students there was one Jew by the name of Tokhterman. He learned diligently and well. For years he suffered ridicule, mockery, loneliness, and often also attacks. In the last few months—during the summer of 1937—just before final exams, the situation became unbearable. On one occasion his colleagues put him in such dire straits that he jumped out of the window and went home. A teacher from the school, who thought highly of him, wrote him a letter and assured him that she guarantees his well-being, but Tokhterman never crossed the school's threshold again. One can imagine how much suffering and torment accumulated in this young Jewish man when he decided to run away from a school to which he had given the three best years of his life. No, he did not run away; he jumped out of a window because the danger to him was also physical.

{Undated (1937)}

2. Pogrom gunpowder

It would be false, of course, to claim that there are pogroms happening in Poland. It would likewise be untrue to say that Poland's Jewish population is dominated by a pogrom mood. It is true, however, that not one day passes in Poland without someone beating Jews somewhere. It is also true that in that place where they are beating Jews, or on that street (if it is in a large city) where they are assailing Jews and roughing them up, a pogrom mood does dominate. Jews are afraid to be seen in the streets; they hide or organize self-defence; delegations run and plead with the authorities to restrain the rampaging hooligans. In sum, there is a typical pogrom atmosphere.

There is a Ukrainian saying, "*Ne umer Danilo, a bolyachka yego zadavila.*" It means "Danilo did not die, but the pain crushed him." This is also the distinction between pogroms and simply beating Jews in different places each day, between a pogrom mood dominating the entire country and a pogrom atmosphere poisoning life in individual places.

Let us just consider the facts for the last couple of weeks, which can be considered much calmer than the couple of weeks around the High Holy Days. Perhaps the hooligans worked so actively during the end of Elul[1] and the days between Rosh Hashanah and Yom Kippur in order to sufficiently break Jews' hearts and better prepare them to stand before God Almighty. After all, the hooligans cannot be expected to know that even without broken bones, Polish Jews' hearts are sufficiently broken for them to lament and cry before God during the Days of Awe. During the festivals, however, on *Simchat Torah*,[2] when Jews are not supposed to have broken hearts at all, why did they feel it necessary to break their bones?

Here are the facts. On 23 October 1935 delegations arrived in Warsaw

---

1 {The final month of the Jewish calendar, leading up to Rosh Hashanah.}
2 {The Jewish holiday that celebrates the conclusion of the annual cycle of public Torah readings.}

from the towns of Klobutsk and Triskolask, near Tshenstokhov. They complained to the Ministry of the Interior that for weeks the Endeks had been beating, tormenting, chasing, and persecuting the Jewish population. The Jews from Klobutsk provided a list of 150 Jews who had been beaten and wounded, while the Jews from Triskolask had no more than sixty people beaten.

Was there a pogrom in these places? Did a pogrom mood dominate there?

I will not undertake to pass judgement on this question. I believe, however, that the best answer would be offered by the battered ribs and broken bones of the victims and by the terrified eyes and dejected souls of the people frightened of the Endek hooligans' clubs and knives, although they have yet to taste them.

Here is news from Lublin on 15 October: in the streets, and especially near Jewish stores, literally right in front of their doors and in full view of the Jewish shopkeepers, people handed out leaflets reading "Poland is for Poles! Remember, don't buy from Jews!"

The proprietor of a haberdashery, a Mr. Fuks, summoned a police officer. They led this Jewish man off to the precinct and composed a report accusing him of "disturbing the peace." It goes without saying that the next day they carried on handing out the same boycott leaflets without a care in the world. Not all patriotic Lubliners, however, are satisfied with merely calling on people not to buy from Jews. Lublin is also home to more active and energetic patriots who beat Jews; the sixty-year-old teacher, Moyshe Sobyarski, recently died due to hooligans' blows.

How is the mood in Lublin? Is it a pogrom mood, like in Ukraine in 1919, like in Kishinev in 1903, like in Gomel that same year? Certainly not! Still, the Jews of Lublin are not exactly cheerful. No matter how much you reassure them that in tsarist Russia and in Ukraine under Petliura things were much, much worse, they refuse to be comforted. Jews have this nasty tendency. They hate even little "pogromlets;" they won't even put up with one Jew murdered and a couple dozen wounded.

A day after *Simchat Torah*, a severely wounded Jewish man, Yehoyshue Povonzek, was brought to the Warsaw Jewish Hospital from the town of Dobre. It turned out that this man had been returning with many other

Jews from performing *hakafot*.[3] They were attacked by hooligans and brutally beaten. More than twenty Jews were wounded, several severely and Yehoyshue Povonzek life-threateningly. You can imagine how much joy they derived in Dobre from the festival of *Simchat Torah*, and how the town's Jewish community spent the last days of *Sukkot*.

Not far from Nove-Myasto, on the road to Warsaw, hooligans attacked a group of Revisionists[4] who were returning from a gathering in Pultusk {Pułtusk}. One hooligan stabbed Zemel Yokovitsh in the heart with a knife, killing him instantly. Hersh Tshesla was severely wounded.

For over a month, the Endek hooligans have been terrorizing the Jewish population of Lodz. During the Sejm {parliament} elections, it was simply impossible to walk through the streets near the Endeks' meeting hall. They beat, chased, insulted, and roughed up Jews. In many Jewish shops, they poured oil and carbolic acid over the merchandise. The Jewish retailers complained and sent delegations to the authorities, but the hooligans were not afraid. They carried out their work worry-free and with great zeal. It is evident that these are organized, centrally administered gangs at work.

Here is a list of wounded Jewish merchants from just one region of the city, Baluty, the Jewish working-class quarter: Moyshe Dzhalovski, Mendl Yasenberg, Blavat, Grinboym, Rotshteyn, Izbitski, Gliksman, Tukhmakher, and Migut. The attacks in other regions of the city, even in downtown Lodz, on Pilsudskego {Piłsudskiego} and Poludniove {Południowa} and the surrounding streets, were even more murderous. They broke into Jewish bakeries and pastry shops and poured oil on the baked goods. They ran into Jewish butcher shops and doused the meat with carbolic acid.

If you walk through the streets of Lodz, you can see thousands of Jews running—not running away from pogroms, just running—some to take out a loan and some to pay off a promissory note; some to grab a customer and some to sell a package of merchandise; some with a rope around their neck, looking to transport a package and earn twenty *groszy* {pennies}, and some with a mountainous bale of merchandise on their

---

3 {Circular processions performed in the synagogue on *Hoshana Rabbah* (the final day of *Sukkot*) and *Simchat Torah*.}

4 {Revisionist Zionism was a militaristic Zionist movement founded by Vladimir (Ze'ev) Jabotinsky in 1925. It emphasized Jewish sovereignty over a state on both sides of the Jordan River.}

shoulders and a happy face because the twenty *groszy* is already in their pocket. A rustling, seething, humming, racing mass, as if rhythmically beating. A living! Bread! Food for wife and children!

It is difficult for foreign eyes to recognize that many of these crooked and twisted backs have been struck more than once by Endek clubs. They have had no time to pause and consider the true purpose and deeper significance of these clubs that beat Jewish backs. It would not occur to anyone to claim that pogroms are happening in Lodz or that a pogrom mood dominates there.

So what exactly *is* happening in Lodz, when every day they beat a score of Jews and destroy merchandise in Jewish stores? What should we call this? Let us consider more facts.

In Slonim, hooligans attacked a Jewish shopkeeper named Polonsk, poked out one of her eyes, and left a hole in her skull. They regularly beat Jews in the public garden, and they recently pelted a group of Jewish doctors with stones as they were walking through it.

Five Jews were traveling from Nashelsk {Nasielsk} to Warsaw with a wagon of potatoes. Young peasants assailed them, beat up the Jews, and destroyed the potatoes. Young peasants—that means that they are "educated" and probably read pogrom leaflets.

In the town of Vyelun {Wieluń}, twenty-three Jewish children went on strike and refused to go to school. Why? First, because their Polish classmates would treat them to slaps and punches as they arrived and departed. The children would come home tear-soaked and distressed. Second, because the teacher himself gave them a lovely welcome on the first day of class. He cried out, "We don't want any Jewish children!" and the Polish children joined in: "We don't want to learn with kikes!"

Krasinski Garden is in the centre of Warsaw's Jewish ghetto, right by Nalevki Street. Jewish children play there, pale, hungry, and skinny, but still children with children's appetites for running, jumping, and playing. Last week, eight Jewish children went into a Jewish editorial office to complain that they were being beaten and chased away and prevented from enjoying running around freely.

On the first day of Rosh Hashanah, a gang of hooligans attacked kibbutz Haganim in Radom.[5] They used clubs and stones to assault

---

5 {Zionist youth movements in Poland established collective agricultural settlements to prepare members for emigration to Palestine.}

three pioneers whom they found on the kibbutz, causing them severe injuries. The hooligans were not caught.

In central Warsaw, a Jewish man, Arn Himelshteyn, was walking along Chlodne {Chłodna} Street. A hooligan assaulted him, beating him with brass knuckles and poking out his eye. There are frequent attacks against Jews in this neighbourhood, but nobody ever gets caught. On the Jewish streets in Warsaw—Novolipie {Nowolipie}, Mila {Miła}, Zamenhof—the watchmen's children, all of whom are Christians, have started a trend of beating Jews in the evenings before the streetlamps are turned on: old people, married women, children, young women. The Jewish workers demonstrated to the hooligans in no uncertain terms that Novolipie and Mila Streets are not Chlodne, which is located beyond the Jewish ghetto and cannot be as effectively defended.

Upon becoming acquainted with the facts, which we have not even come close to exhausting, one feels compelled to draw several conclusions and pose several questions.

First, the pogrom wave has seized all regions of Poland, from Slonim to Lodz, from Poznan region to Vilna region, from the smallest towns and villages to the largest cities, including the capital. One gets the impression that a huge quantity of pogrom gunpowder has accumulated, and at the first opportunity this gunpowder could explode, leading to the greatest destruction and the most tragic results.

Second, large groups of people prowl around this gunpowder, led by a main party of arsonists and purveyors of explosives, who work energetically to amass the gunpowder and expedite its explosion.

Third, aside from organized workers, there is virtually no organized Polish social force that stands in any degree of opposition to the pogrom agitation and the pogrom wave, which is swelling and flooding the country.

Fourth, the local authorities respond variously to attacks against Jews. In tens of cases, the assailants are not caught. In tens of cases, they are so lightly and trivially punished that the criminals feel almost encouraged to carry on beating Jews and cracking their skulls. However, there are many cases in which the police are sufficiently active in identifying the criminals and the judges are sufficiently severe in punishing the hooligans. The police everywhere are sufficiently active to prevent attacks from expanding into large-scale pogroms.

Whether they do so out of love toward Jews or out of hatred toward the pogromists, who oppose the current regime, is an important question, but the answer is clear enough. They allow the hooligans to live it up a little, not wanting to make a big deal out of a couple of holes in Jewish skulls or the destruction of ten or so Jews' merchandise. However, they keep a watchful eye on these organized gangs of hooligans to keep them from fanning the flames of the pogrom fire too much and transforming the Jewish conflagration into a political conflagration.

Fifth, based on the previous point, the attitude and tactics of the central government with respect to the pogroms also become clear. They become even clearer when it is established that murdering a Jew or wounding several Jews carries a much lighter punishment than, for example, distributing Communist leaflets. They do not allow explicit calls for pogroms or for the murder and destruction of Jews, but they allow Jews to be blamed for all sorts of misery and misfortune in Poland, for all the poverty and hunger in the countryside and city, for all the destitution and deprivation of the population. They permit the accusation that Jews are actively seeking to destroy Poland and corrupt the Polish nation. I feel it unnecessary to add that, practically speaking, this is pogrom agitation.

And now a few questions. First, what is Jewish society doing to explain to the better parts of Polish society (which, although minimal, do exist) the great danger posed by these pogrom waves, which are poisoning the entire atmosphere, and which are bound to eventually become a danger to Poland itself?

Second, what is Jewish society doing to compel the Polish government to stop the pogrom agitation and prevent the poison from spreading further, which would inevitably and tragically end in large-scale pogroms?

Third, what is Jewish society doing to compel the government to adopt severe measures against individual attacks, against small pogroms, and against individual cases of murder and maiming, since these will without a doubt ultimately result in mass murders and large pogroms?

Fourth, what is Jewish society doing to organize itself and speak out in a coordinated manner against the pogrom rehearsals of a political party that openly preaches pogroms as a means of political struggle and declares its goal to be Hitler's program, but in a more extreme form since, after all, Poland has seven or eight times as many Jews as Germany?

And fifth, what is Jewish society doing to create a common front on at least one matter, the matter of self-defence against pogroms and against preparations for the major slaughter to which the Endeks look forward with such great hopes?

It must be acknowledged that to all of these questions, there is a single tragic and horrifying answer. At this very moment of danger, Polish Jews are torn and splintered, divided and dispersed like never before.

13 November 1935

3. The Minsk-Mazovyetsk pogrom

The antisemitic atmosphere is so tense and heated that the smallest of sparks is enough to set the fire ablaze. Everyone's nerves, both Poles' and Jews', are so taut and aggravated that at the first sign of fire, they go running to the ends of the earth, losing all self-control and reason—all the more so when there are thousands of arsonists standing at the ready, just waiting for the opportunity to initiate the spark and fan it into a conflagration. This is especially so when Polish life is so aggravated and disorganized, and poverty spreading so quickly, that even nerves of steel are unable to withstand it.

Is it necessary to add that there are thousands of distinct causes that are rattling Jewish nerves even more, literally ruining the Jewish soul, turning us into physical and mental invalids, robbing us of the bare minimum amount of rest and security necessary for a person to live? Is it necessary to describe how miserable it is to be afraid of every rustle, every movement among the surrounding masses, every tremble the nation makes for entirely different reasons? After all, there stand at the ready large, organized parties with an interest in directing every movement among the masses, each awakened thought, all of the awakened fury, toward the heads of the Jews. Unfortunately, they are largely successful.

It is thus no surprise at all that these master pogromists find it so easy to incite the rabble against Jews when a misfortune really does take place.

Precisely such a misfortune, which led to tens of people wounded and hundreds of families ruined, took place in Minsk-Mazovyetsk. A sick Jew, a madman, a maniac, a wretched cripple, shot a Christian man to death. Of all people, this was a Christian who had good relationships with Jews, who was respected by the city's entire population, and who was a genuinely decent person. His wife, despite the great misfortune she suffered, deeply regretted the tragic events. She understood very well that it was wild, barbaric, bestial to punish an entire city's population for an act by a madman.

Nevertheless, the master pogromists simply needed a little something to latch onto; they were eagerly awaiting the spark they could fan into a conflagration capable of annihilating a city's worth of people. Their work was a dazzling success.

Here is the first list of the severely wounded: Khane Zhelyazke, Leyb Nayman, Khaim Kornfeld, Arn Feldman, Tsivye Shpigel, Shmuel Zaydentreger, Yankev Granatovitsh, Leyb Rozenberg, Sore Mikanovska, Zishe Altmed, Rakhmiel Ayzenshteyn, Yisroel Popovski, Yankev Grinberg, Khaye Perkal, Velvl Biblyazh, Shmuel Kagan, Yoysef Mlinski, Mrs. Mlinski, Leyb Berman, Mordkhe Mints, Yankev Daugus, Ber Nagelevski, Ber Rozenblat (seventy years old), Efroim Furmanski (sixty-two years old), and Ester Goldshteyn. In total, twenty-five people severely wounded.

Of course, this is not even half of all of the people wounded. There is still no confirmed list of victims, not even of people harmed *physically*. It is still unknown whether anyone was killed. Likewise, it is unknown how many stores were looted or how many houses and stores were burned.

The Polish Jews have many caregivers who are competing intensely amongst themselves, racing to outdo each other and demonstrate how deeply they care for the Jewish community. Members of four or five committees run to the authorities, each declaring that they are in charge. The result is one I would wish not only on Hitler, but also on his Polish students.

The final calculation is clear enough: the entire city is in ruins—the Jewish part, of course. Hundreds of houses have had all of their windows shattered, their furniture smashed, their cushions torn apart, and all of the feathers released from their bedding. Hundreds of stores have been looted and tens of houses burned. Our large masses of beggars have been joined by several hundred, and perhaps even a couple thousand, fresh ones. The crop of Jewish beggars is growing: beggars from the boycott, beggars from the economic crisis, beggars fleeing the villages, beggars from towns with pogroms, beggars from towns awaiting pogroms.

In recent days, hundreds of Jews can be seen drifting around the courtyard of the Jewish communal leadership, trudging from one Jewish committee or editorial office to the next, seeking help, begging for bread, longing for a place to sleep, a place to rest and forget the nightmare somewhat. These are all yesterday's *bourgeoisie*, who themselves distributed bread to the poor and contributed to charitable societies.

Fig. 6 Victims of the Minsk-Mazovyetsk pogrom, June 1936. Wikimedia, public domain, https://commons.wikimedia.org/wiki/File:Ofiary_pogromu_w_Mi%C5%84sku_Mazowieckim_czerwiec_1936.jpg

The panic that had seized the Jewish population of Minsk-Mazovyetsk is indescribable. The atmosphere had been tense since the first of May, when the *Po'ale Tsiyon* member Tsilikh was killed and several Jews were severely wounded, and one hooligan was also stabbed. The Jewish population had no rest this entire time, since the Endeks, in full view of the local police, conducted wild agitation for a pogrom and revenge. It seemed to them that they had paid too steep a price: one whole hooligan wounded for one Jew killed and five or six wounded. Throughout this time, they had been threatening to settle the account. Now, God had practically tossed down from heaven a golden opportunity to wreak destruction, inflict wounds on Jewish bodies and souls, foment panic in tens of towns around Minsk-Mazovyetsk, and rob the entire Polish Jewish population of their sense of calm and security.

As the atmosphere in Minsk-Mazovyetsk grew hotter; as people sensed ever more keenly that just an hour from Warsaw, practically under the central government's nose, people were beating Jews day and night without intervention; as the fleeing of hundreds of families dragged on, the hooligans in every city and town grew bolder, and the Jewish population grew ever more panicked and uncertain.

Minsk-Mazovyetsk is, after all, only one hour from Warsaw. Over the course of a single hour, more than enough police could have been brought in to establish order. In this instance, nowhere near the entire Christian population participated in the pogrom. On the contrary, a very significant portion was against the pogrom. True, not actively against it, but against it nonetheless. And that is not even counting the workers. There are tens of known cases in which Christians hid Jews and even risked their lives and houses. In fact, the hooligans set fire to several Christian houses and threatened revenge against Christians who hid Jews. A few tens of police officers could have chased off the whole gang of hooligans and, if necessary, arrested them. Despite this, the situation continued for an entire week. Only now are people gradually beginning to return, although they are afraid to open their stores and they remain locked indoors, sleeping in their clothes if they sleep at all.

For four days, news floods in from Minsk-Mazovyetsk, as if from a battlefield, although a very peculiar and perhaps modern battlefield. The enemy has fled or lies hidden in the attics and cellars; the aggressor, however, does not lose his desire for war, so he exacts vengeance against cushions, featherbeds, windows, cupboards, merchandise, chairs, and tables. He smashes and destroys everything he can get his hands on. The third party, the one that in the first place should never have allowed war to break out among citizens who, despite their differing statuses, belong to one state—this actual master of the country and custodian of order makes a face as though he is very displeased by the civil war. He gives orders and pretends to be on the verge of eradicating all the malicious spirits and agents of destruction, while the pogrom carries on for four days—and the panic, an entire week.

These are the kind of peculiarly modern things that can happen in today's Poland. This goes to show how secure one's life is in Poland. This is the extent to which one can think of a livelihood or a tomorrow, or any future at all.

Both the audacity of the pogromists and the trepidation of the Jews are spreading like a plague. In the town of Kolbyel {Kołbiel}, they smashed the windows of Jewish houses and stores. They wounded several Jews and stabbed a man named Rozenshteyn with a knife, causing severe injuries.

In Skale {Skała}, Eastern Galicia, Ukrainian fascists smashed several hundred windows of Jewish houses, and several Jews were injured there too; one sustained a severe wound after being shot with a revolver.

In Vaver {Wawer}, near Warsaw, they stabbed the son of Rabbi Kestenberg with a knife. He had to be taken to the hospital. At the same time, they smashed all the windows of his apartment and the study and prayer house.

In Radzimin {Radzymin}, hooligan military recruits started beating Jewish recruits who were standing naked, ready to appear before the medical commission. This was the first lesson given to future Jewish fighters for the Polish fatherland.

In Dobra, Volomin {Wołomin}, Kartshev {Karczew}, Vlokhi {Włochy}—all around Warsaw—terror is running rampant. People are beating, robbing, smashing windows, wounding Jews' heads and making their lives so miserable they are utterly disgusted and fed up.

In Warsaw itself, the capital city, the centre of Europe, in full view of the Polish authorities, there is a constant pogrom. In Mokotov {Mokotów}, a Warsaw suburb, they broke into a shop owned by a Jewish man named Rozenberg, shouting, "Today you're going to be turned into a mountain of ash!" When the woman in charge started screaming, they kicked her so hard with a boot in the stomach that she lost consciousness. In the Saxon Garden, the assaults on Jews have continued. They beat them with clubs and iron bars. It would be no exaggeration to say that a minimum of seven or eight hundred Jews have been wounded in the last year in Warsaw, one at a time, and there are hundreds with holes in their skulls. We have the names of more than a hundred severely wounded people in Warsaw. The mildly wounded make no reports.

The prime minister's speech before the Sejm was like salt in our wounds. The new prime minister tried cosying up to the Jews. He said that he would not allow anyone to beat Jews, but this was the kind of cosiness that could make your vision grow dark. Things have indeed grown so dark and miserable that everyone you meet groans and sighs and comes to the general conclusion that now the pogroms are really about to get started.

The prime minister said, "Economic struggle by all means, but no mistreatment." This is also the wording of the antisemitic newspaper *Dziennik Narodowy* as it calls every day for a pogrom against Jewish pockets. The simple masses, however, do not get bogged down in the details. If someone says to them, "pogrom against Jewish pockets," they understand that chasing Jews out of the market square, preventing peasants from buying from Jews, preventing Jews from selling in the market, and compelling them to leave town altogether is obviously the best pogrom against Jewish pockets; the impact is swift and powerful. Indeed, if the Jews will not leave by choice, they must be shown the way with stones, clubs, iron bars, fires, and revolvers. Otherwise, the economic struggle and the pogrom against Jewish pockets will yield no results.

If a prime minister declares from the dais before parliament that it is acceptable to engage in economic struggle against Jews, rather than equitable competition, the simple antisemite can reach the logical conclusion that the best struggle is a club and a knife. This is how it works in practice, as can be seen every day. The government has now been in office for three weeks. It is a strong government—and the pogrom wave is spreading and intensifying; the attacks are transforming into outright slaughters; the pogromists feel free and exuberant as they carry out their work with diligence and zeal. The new government does not utter a word, not to mention actually doing anything!

Jews thus go around with their heads down, with wounds in their hearts, with extinguished eyes, with endless sorrow in their souls!

From where and when will help come?[1]

20 June 1936

---

1 {A reference to Psalm 121:1}.

4. The Pshitik pogrom

The "Jewish pogrom"

Jews apparently carried out a pogrom in Pshitik against "goyim" {gentiles}! Did you know about this already? We did not know about it in Poland either, and yet I have the indictment right in front of my eyes and am reading it in astonishment. It turns out that the Jews of Pshitik have carried out a pogrom against the Christians! The Pshitik Jews, who had been tormented and persecuted for months leading up to the pogrom, who were afraid to turn up at the market with their merchandise, who were terrorized by every little Christian boy—these very Pshitik Jews, on the infamous date of 9 March 1936, during the fair, when there were thousands of peasant villagers in town, threw stones at the Christians and beat them with clubs and iron rods. Not only did they beat them; they also shot them many times. With their shooting and beating of "goyim," the Jews provoked an attack.

For this reason, the indictment begins with the fourteen Jewish defendants. The Jews face harsh sentences. There is not one word about the fact that they were compelled to protect and defend themselves against a bestial mob, an agitated crowd that had already pillaged and beaten and was prepared to kill. Of course, it is difficult to establish precisely when a person has the right to defend himself with the most extreme means. Is it in the beginning, when he is first attacked, when he still has strength and the genuine opportunity to save himself from the wild assailants? Or is it only when he is lying wounded, defeated, and unable to move that he has the right to reach for his revolver? The investigative authorities ought to have asked themselves this question and determined a clear answer: did the couple of young Jewish men shoot when the pogrom was already in progress or before it began? It is indeed unimportant whether the pogromists killed the Minkovski family before or after the shooting. The pogromists would in any case have killed, if not the Minkovskis, then others. The indictment itself proves that the pogromists were satisfied when they caught the scent of Jewish blood, when they saw the blood-drenched bodies of the Minkovskis, who were by that point not even recognizable.

What exactly *is* the indictment's approach to the events in Pshitik? It begins with the fact that several peasants resisted the efforts of the police to create order. It would, of course, be logical here to dwell in detail upon the events, to paint a picture of the pogrom, of the mob gone wild, of the agitators inciting them and calling for pogroms and murder, of the attacks on Jews and the beatings—in short, a picture of the true pogrom. It would then make sense to describe how Jews tried to defend themselves, some with revolvers and others with clubs. However, the indictment's author takes an entirely different approach. He drags the Jews out into the foreground; he places those who had the audacity to defend themselves front and centre. The indictment begins as follows:

> The Jews, Yankl Avrom Khaberberg, Leyzer Feldberg, Yankl Zeyde, Refoel Honik, Moyshe Fersht, Shoyel Kengel, Moyshe Tsuker, Leyb Lenge, Yitskhok Bande, and Yitskhok Fridman face the following accusation: At the same time as the clash between the police and the peasants, they attacked the peasants, who were rushing to drive home, beating them with clubs and other instruments, throwing stones at them, and thereby causing Jozef Szymanski head wounds that led to mental health issues, and wounding many other peasants, who sustained bruises and edema.

This introduction alone already turns the whole case backward. Peasants are racing to escape the market, peasants are rushing home, and Jews turn up and start beating them. Innocent little lambs are attacked by wild Jewish beasts who will not let the lambs go home in peace and quiet! That's what the Pshitik Jews are capable of! And that is just the beginning. The indictment continues: "The Jews are further accused of *intending to murder the peasants* who were rushing to leave the market, since they shot at them! However, they failed several times to hit their target, since only three peasants were seriously injured, one of them life-threateningly."

Again, the peasants are bothering nobody, laying a hand on nobody; they are nice, quiet, peaceful little Pshitik Christians. The poor guys just want to run home to their wives and children as quick as they can. The previously mentioned ten Jews, however, are armed with revolvers and ready and willing to murder. These hostile Jews shoot with the clear intention to murder, but they do not succeed.

Then come additional specific accusations against individual Jews. Sholem Leska is accused of "attempting to murder the peasants who were walking around the market, shooting from the window of his house and murdering one peasant."

Thus, again, the peasants are walking calmly around the market, and the Jew Leska shoots from his window, simply for the purpose of murder. However, this same indictment establishes that the window had been shattered. Well, who smashed the window through which Leska subsequently shot? If the peasants were simply strolling around peacefully, why on earth were Jews' windowpanes smashed?

Next comes the accusation against Yankl Bornshteyn, who also attempted to murder peasants. He shot, but missed.

Only after the indictment finishes with the Jews, the main criminals and primary defendants, does it move on to the forty accused Christians, who, "after the peasant had been shot dead," attacked Jewish houses in groups, "shattered doors and windows, broke into the houses, destroyed all of the furniture, smashed everything they came across, beat all the Jews, murdered the Jews Yoysef and Khaya Minkovski, seriously wounded five Jews, and more mildly wounded several additional Jews."

Everything is now clear. If the Jews had not beaten the peasants, who were rushing home, if the Jews had not shot at the peasants who were walking peacefully around the market, there would have been no pogrom at all, and Pshitik would have remained some anonymous, grubby town, rather than becoming world-famous. It is clear who the guilty party is.

This same spirit will undoubtedly carry over into the trial set to begin on the second of June in Radom, in which fourteen Jews and forty Christians stand accused. However, the former are accused of crimes carrying sentences of five to ten years imprisonment, whereas the latter face far less serious sentences.

If one sets the indictment aside and starts reading the justification of the accusations, one sees that the writer got so carried away by the facts in front of his eyes that he forgot what he was supposed to be justifying and inadvertently let a lot of truth slip out. He remembers his objective from time to time and emphasizes that Jews armed themselves, that Jews bought revolvers in Radom, that Jews were even seen to have brought nine revolvers. Among the Christian population, people were saying that Jews were preparing for a general attack. The overall picture, however, even as it is painted in the justification of the indictment, ultimately reveals the truth that Jews had been living in a state of panic for months, that the Endeks had long ago implemented a boycott of Jewish businesses, using force to prevent people from buying from Jews, that Jewish windowpanes had long since been at their mercy, and that a pogrom mood could be felt in the air that day.

Let us consider just a few sketches taken straight from the justification of the indictment. People broke into the home of Yankl Bornshteyn through the windows. They smashed the wardrobe, table, and chairs, and struck Bornshteyn with clubs and stones. The investigation found forty-eight stones in the home, many of them large. So when did Bornshteyn shoot—before they threw the stones or after? While the pogromists were in the home, they were obviously not throwing stones. This clearly indicates that Bornshteyn wanted to chase off the pogromists by shooting—that is, of course, if Bornshteyn even shot at all, which he himself denies.

Sholem Leska confessed to shooting and killing the peasant, and his fate is very grave indeed.

Even in the dry, bureaucratic description, the scene in the home of Feyge Shukh makes a powerful impression. She hid her eight children in the attic and stood by the door to her home, heroically fighting against a crowd of peasants who beat her with clubs, inflicted three severe head wounds, fractured her spine, and caused many bruises to her chest and back. She saved her children though.

Here is another moving scene: in the heat of the pogrom—in the greatest peril, a seventy-year-old Jewish woman named Yokheved Palant went out into the street to look for her children. The pogromists surrounded her and beat her brutally, causing numerous head wounds.

A shocking impression is left by the description of how people broke into the home of the cobbler Minkovski, beat him cruelly and brutally over the head with crowbars, and dragged his children out from under the bed. The cobbler's wife fell under the blows and the cobbler himself was transformed into a pool of blood.

As you read the bureaucratic description, you see before your eyes Kishinev, Homel, Bialystok, and tens of other major cities where pogroms took place during the tsarist period. The same cruelty, the same sadism, the same brutality and bestiality, the same loss of human appearance and human feelings.

At the same time, there was something that brought comfort. Jews, it appears, defended themselves! The Jews of Pshitik did not allow themselves to be slaughtered like sheep! The indictment does exaggerate, but something did take place. There were young Jews who were ready to make the greatest sacrifice to prevent our name from being disgraced and our honour from being mocked!

5 June 1936

The scene is set

I want to begin my report on the Pshitik trial with the following picture. More than 400 witnesses had to be sworn in. They were brought into the hall in groups. First come four groups of gentiles—320 witnesses, mostly young men with healthy, rustic faces. Dressed in boots, they enter the hall resolutely and confidently, almost joyfully, almost brashly. They answer prosecutor's questions loudly, insolently, provocatively, almost belligerently. So it goes, one group after another—the floor trembling under the 320 pairs of healthy boots, the stamping of their metal heels, the scraping of their thick soles.

Here come the eighty Jewish witnesses. First, the five orphans of the murdered Minkovskis, between six and fourteen years old. After them, the grandmother, over seventy years old, and ten aged, stooped men, old women so tiny and short you can hardly see them—a whole group of men and women, shabby, faded, dejected, hesitant, with lost faces and extinguished eyes. They look almost like a pack of beggars and panhandlers, at least like a group of wanderers, arriving from a long and difficult journey, tired, far from home, depleted, longing for rest and security.

I was standing very close to the judges' table and could observe the impression that the arrival of this group of witnesses made on everyone—the judges, the lawyers, and the journalists: crushing, shocking! It was a deeply unpleasant picture. The contrast with the young peasants' suntanned faces and tall figures was too great. Everyone was seized by entirely different feelings. Against their will, a thought flashed through everyone's minds, even the viciously antisemitic lawyers': before our eyes stand the beaten and the tormented, the harassed and the hounded.

At that moment, the trial acquired its true historical significance, and all the investigations, speculations, interrogations, and pains to pick out the guilty and the innocent seemed superfluous, somehow foolish and absurd. It is clear, after all, that the strong are the ones who do the beating. It is even clearer that the weak are the ones who get beaten. What was the point of going through such long, drawn-out ceremonies?

In truth, the matter is not quite so simple. These weak grandfathers and weary fathers, these stooped grandmothers and wrinkled mothers have children. Not all Jewish youth are little and skinny these days, and even when they are little and skinny, they are strong with an entirely different will and sense of courage, not with a passive will for God to rescue and redeem, but an active will to stop others, here and now, from spitting in their face. Their will is to respond to an attack not with prayers and petitions to God, not with begging and pleading, but with a bullet.

In this sense, the figure of the Jewish tailor boy Leska is truly symbolic. He is not yet twenty years old, short and skinny, near sighted and bespectacled. He confessed that he had fired a revolver. He hit a peasant and killed him instantly. We are not judging now on the third day of the trial whether Leska ought to have fired at the moment he did. But Leska from Pshitik, still in a long kaftan, just a couple years out of the *yeshiva*, a member of the Mizrakhi religious Zionist movement, a young man who had never seen or heard from his father or grandfather about weapons, about shooting, about revolvers and rifles—this young man was armed and ready to fight for himself, his parents, his little brothers and sisters.

The forty-three Christian accused are practically all cut from the same cloth—peasant youths, the first generation to don city clothes: shoes, a tie, a half-white collar, an ironed suit, hair combed with a part. This is the first generation of peasants to graduate elementary school. They arrived to occupy the market and fair sites, and they attacked the Jews.

When the chairman starts asking each of the accused about their name and past, the difference between the Jewish and non-Jewish small-town youth immediately becomes apparent.

"Have you ever been to prison?" the chairman asks, and almost all of the Jews answer, "No!" A few have served time, but for Communism. Many of the Christian have served time for stealing laundry or a horse, for fighting, or for assaults against Jews. Theft, brawling, and assaults against Jews—these are the commonest crimes in villages and in small towns which are themselves practically villages or are located right next to a village.

One must not overgeneralize, of course. Poland has no shortage of Jewish thieves and louts who go around with knives, ready to stab someone at the slightest confrontation. Nonetheless, both these types are less common among Jews. The main point is that here in the courtroom sit two highly disparate groups. On one side, assailants, brawlers, hooligans, people who allowed themselves to be convinced that Jews are responsible for all misfortunes. On the other side, people who, in the worst-case scenario, wanted to defend themselves, tried to defend themselves, refused to hide in the attic or basement listening to the cries and screams of women and children being beaten.

I say "in the worst-case scenario" because the accused Jews all deny that there was a self-defence organization, that they had several revolvers, and they assert that they wanted to defend themselves against hooligans and murderers, that every person has a right to self-defence.

The disparity was likewise glaring as they answered the chairman's questions. The brawlers were audacious, sure of themselves, even a little impudent. Several even dared to say that they were not willing to answer now and reserved the right to speak later. The chairman of the court's angry words were of no use—they remained stubbornly silent. The Jewish accused were not entirely sure of themselves, with fear on their faces and distrust of those in whose hands their fate laid. At the same time, they conducted themselves with dignity and intelligence. Their responses got straight to the point and they refused to be twisted around by the antisemitic lawyers.

Let us briefly consider the judges and lawyers, and we will then have before us all the actors in the tragedy currently playing out in the Radom courtroom.

The chairman of the court, for the time being, makes a very favourable impression. His conduct is impartial, serious, and honest. He made a speech to the Christian witnesses that might serve as a key to how he wants to conduct the trial, and perhaps also the trial's outcome. He demanded from them the truth, because only through truth can the hatred and hostility between different segments of the population be reduced. There have been enough victims, and the discord has come at a heavy price; every witness must strive not to exact revenge, but to help establish peaceful relations by telling the truth. The chairman spoke these words with a resolute and commanding voice. Unfortunately, this did not make much of an impression on the Christian witnesses, and they continued to conduct themselves in an impudent and provocative manner. One got the impression that there were more pogromists, and more dangerous ones, among the witnesses than the accused. The chairman also made a speech for the Jewish witnesses, but in a somewhat different style. Here, he felt it necessary to mention that an oath without a rabbi is still an oath, since God is everywhere.

At the same time, however, the chairman has two court assessors {investigating magistrates} who are noted antisemites, and they make no effort to hide their antipathy toward the Jewish accused.

The Jewish accused are defended by a group of brilliant and widely renowned lawyers. Alongside the Jews Berenson, Ettinger, Margolis, and Kriger, there are the Christians Petruszewicz, Paschalski and Szymanski. Petruszewicz is a lawyer from Vilna, one of the old-time Russian political defenders, a true friend of humanity, a true leftist, and an eminent and esteemed jurist who is also a professor at Vilna University. Paschalski is the president of the Riflemen's Association, an organization of Pilsudski's that plays a major role in Polish political life.

The pogromists are represented by fifteen antisemitic lawyers. Their best lawyers from Warsaw and Lodz, in addition to those from Radom, felt that it was their "moral" duty to come and save the pogromists. From the very first moment, they made it clear that they had come not for money, not for the sake of this or that individual defendant, but to save the Polish nation from the Jewish leech. It is a fact that not one of them is accepting any payment. They have come here to spend whole days sweating in court solely to perform a good deed. In short, they are convinced, tenacious, proficient antisemites. Among them is a rather beautiful young female lawyer, with a pleasant face that is entirely unsuited to the venomous hatred that sprays from her mouth every time she questions a Jewish defendant. She is, however, very active.

The scene has been set; the actors have taken their places. With racing hearts, the Jews of Poland, and perhaps also Jews around the world, snap up every bit of news about what is happening onstage.

19 June 1936

Leyzer Feldberg

The two days that I spent at the Pshitik trial were truly historic days. This was not so much because great heroes appeared and exposed the entire tragic situation of a group of people who are attacked daily, require police protection but do not receive it, and are nevertheless forbidden from defending themselves, and especially from organizing for the purpose of self-defence. Alas, there are no great heroes at the Pshitik trial. Almost all the defendants have set out to prove that they could not have shot, would not have wanted to shoot, and did not even think about beating pogromists. The defendant Leska represents an exception in this regard, but we are afraid that this is only because he has ended up in a situation in which he is forced to confess and plead self-defence against assailants as his motive. Leska, as is known, shot from a window and killed a peasant, and he is facing the heaviest sentence.

Let us be impartial toward all the Jewish defendants, who sit before the court in terror and anxiety as they insult and disgrace their own honour. On the day of the pogrom, they conducted themselves far more heroically, far more courageously, far more admirably and honourably. More than one hooligan's back got a taste of a Jew's club or iron bar. At that moment, they behaved as healthy, normal people ought to when they are attacked.

Nonetheless, the two days of the trial were historic. The proceedings were raised to a high level insofar as the pain and grief not of individual people but of all three million Polish Jews, drowning in misery, were established.

The credit for all of this is due to an ordinary Jewish man, a very simple man of the type immortalized by Sholem Aleichem in *Tevye the Dairyman*. These simple people, steadfast in their faith, firm in their conscience, intact and unbroken in their nature, candid and generous, unafraid for their own skin and prepared to serve as a sacrifice should the community require it—people like this often become heroes without even realizing that they are speaking or acting heroically, but simply by showing, "This is how I am!" This is the most appealing characteristic of these simple souls; they possess the wisdom of the people, and with this they compel even their enemies to hear them out.

God sent precisely such a man of the people to the trial, someone without pretentions or disguises. He plays his role absolutely naturally and so honestly, so conscientiously, so faithfully to reality, that over these two days he became a central figure. His name has probably remained in your memory from the telegrams: Feldberg! Leyzer Feldberg!

He is a tall man of sixty-eight years. He has a pale face from weeks of sitting under arrest, and several welts on his bare head. He is hard of hearing, and for this reason his entire figure, especially his face, appears constantly tense and strained. He began to draw attention from the very first day. His entire appearance seemed to cry out that a country where this old man could sit under arrest for assaulting and beating innocent peasants is without a doubt under the rule of arbitrariness, anarchy, lawlessness, disorder, and chaos. As soon as he answered the first formal questions from the chairman of the court, one could sense in this man a special inner certainty, a special purity and strength of conscience. He stepped up to the courtroom lectern with a calm intensity and answered—and his answers had to be believed! On the second day of the trial, he became unwell and had to be excused from the courtroom. Today, however, on the fourth day of the trial, he is being questioned.

This questioning has brought us honour and pride. This sixty-eight-year-old Jewish man declares openly, proudly, courageously, loudly, nearly shouting, that if he had at that moment had a weapon, he would have shot it. He walks right up close to the judge and shouts straight into his face: "Even if you, Your Honour, were to harm me, I would still defend myself!"

This makes a profound impression. More interesting, provocative, and powerful, however, is what he goes on to tell. He describes, almost poetically, how he belongs to one union—the union of the patriarch Abraham! The children of this union stood at the base of Mount Sinai and were the first to hear God's voice, which commanded: thou shalt not murder, thou shalt not steal! These commandments of God remain this union's holiest values to this day. This is the introduction that allows him to conclude that the Jews of Pshitik, children of Abraham, did not bother anyone and were happy when they were left to work and live in peace. "If only there were no knives and no clubs, the town would have been peaceful and calm," Feldberg repeats several times. With a calm but deeply moving voice, he describes how they began to put the knives and clubs to work, how they even beat peasants who dared go up to a Jew's street stall, how they transformed the town into a hell and the market days into days of anguish and catastrophe.

Jews ran to the local authorities and the authorities in Radom. He describes bluntly how the town hall received the Jewish delegation in which he took part, and how the district administrator cynically reassured the Jews that "nobody has been killed yet, after all." In simple words, he describes how they threw the Jewish shoemaker Palant into the river, and how the Jewish delegations demanded protection and pleaded to be saved from murder, but the administrator cracked jokes and claimed that they were just going for the Jews' pockets. "No," old Leyzer Feldberg cries out in the courtroom, "they are going for our heads, not our pockets!" If they leave our heads intact, the gentiles will continue buying from us!

It is impossible to convey the full speech of this courageous man. He is always on cue. He says, "To me, a good priest is better than a bad rabbi." This makes an impression because people can sense the truth of his words.

The following day, however, was even more interesting. Only then did the old man describe how he survived the Pshitik tragedy, which is the tragedy of more than three million Jews. He arrives at the courthouse paler, weaker, more exhausted. People can tell from his face that the old man has slept poorly and that something is tormenting him. He stands up right at the beginning of the session and declares that he has something else to add to what he had said yesterday. Lying on the hard bench in prison, he remembered things he had forgotten to say. The old man then tells in exhaustive detail how they threw the Jewish man Palant into the river, and how he had told the district administrator that they had killed a Jew. At that moment, the chairman, the prosecutor, and the antisemitic lawyer Kowalski exclaim, "There were no Jews killed!" Old Leyzer gazes around with a pair of large, bulging eyes and replies, "But they murdered him!" He says these words very quietly, because the assertion of the aforementioned three apparently hit him hard, but in his gaze is everything: astonishment and contempt.

Pale and agitated, he sits down on the defendants' bench. They question several Christian witnesses. The Christian witness Rogulski, the owner of the house in which the Minkovskis were so bestially murdered, enters. This Rogulski remains absolutely calm as he describes how, when he went into the Minkovskis' room, he found the husband already dead and the wife still dying. When the chairman asks whether he knows the murderers, he replies, "No." At that moment, however, old Feldberg jumps up, runs over to the judges' table and cries out, "I can't take it anymore! I can't take it anymore!" Pointing out Rogulski, he shouts even louder, "It's him; he killed them! He's the murderer!"

Feldberg falls over; several of the accused weep. A recess is called. Feldberg is taken to the hospital.

This scene will remain in the memory of everyone sitting in the courtroom. The antisemitic lawyers, one of whom is the grandchild of a converted Jew, the famous historian Kraushar, can go ahead and smile into their bristly, pure-Polish moustaches; the antisemitic correspondents can go ahead and gnash their teeth as they spread the words of every brutish witness while suppressing the most important moments in the courtroom. Nobody will break free of the influence of Leyzer Feldberg, that man of the people whose every word, whose every movement radiates the wisdom and truth of the folk.

24 June 1936

Jewish and non-Jewish witnesses

One could write a mountain of text about the Pshitik trial. Every day, every hour there are surprises and characteristic qualities. Like in a film, picture after picture flies before one's eyes: witnesses, Jewish and non-Jewish, old gentile and Jewish women, old Jewish and gentile men, young gentile men from the country and small-town ones with combed hair and neckties. An entire gallery of highly interesting, often captivating types, a genuine laboratory or observatory, an observation point for artists as well as sociologists, for those who study the evolution of human society.

One sees here how the village creates its inhabitants, and how the town whittles away at their exterior somewhat, removing their natural simplicity and rustic naïveté, greasing them with small-town pomade, teaching them to look at a newspaper or book, awakening within them appetites and desires, making them crueller and their souls more sinister, with greater cynicism and sharper teeth. The small-town antisemite can thus lie more easily and is no longer so afraid of being lashed in the world to come or penalized in this one, since he is more convinced than the rural antisemite of his party's imminent victory. It is for this reason that he is more insolent. He acts as though he already has half a win in his pocket, or even more. He feels like he is the judges' and prosecutors' future boss and has almost no respect for them whatsoever.

Observing these witnesses with their small-town neckties, one is inadvertently reminded of the trial in Berlin for the pogrom on Kurfürstendamm.[1] Of course, a Berlin hooligan looks entirely different than one from Pshitik, but there is one immense similarity that astounds the observer: the same insolence, built on the secure belief that any minute now, the whip will be in their hand as they assume power. There is a particular cynicism crying out from this insolence, but one must admit that it makes an impression, influencing in particular the judges and the prosecutor. Here in Radom, just like in Berlin, these witnesses, who really ought to be sitting among the accused, speak loudly, imperiously, in a commanding voice.

In our first report about the Pshitik trial, we already drew some comparisons between the Jewish and non-Jewish witnesses. At that point, however, we saw a large crowd of several hundred non-Jews and nearly a hundred Jews. Now we see them one at a time, and only here does it become so clear who is the beater and who the beaten that even the wildly antisemitic lawyers often lose their courage, and when they do dig in their heels and try insistently to twist things so that the Jews were beating and the peasants running away, they fail miserably.

Let us consider another couple of scenes of testimonies from witnesses on both sides.

There were a couple of days when the Jewish witnesses revealed a little corner of that bloody Monday, a date that will be remembered in Jewish history. The corner is small because the witnesses are still living

---

1 {On 12 September 1931, more than 1,000 Nazis attacked Jews on one of Berlin's most famous avenues. It was the first act of mass violence against Jews in Weimar Germany. The police and the judiciary were lenient in their response.}

in Pshitik for the time being, although it is unlikely they will hold out there much longer. They remain immobilized in Pshitik and are afraid to identify the perpetrators. They thus pretend to be blind and ignorant so as to avoid provoking the ferocious enemy.

Here stands Khaye Fridman. During the pogrom, she was holding a small child in her arms. She pleaded with the hooligans not to harm the child, and they did her that favour by directing all of their blows against her. The chairman asks her to approach the defendants' bench and identify the perpetrators. She excuses herself, saying that the blows to her eyes had caused her to see poorly, and she does not want to assume the responsibility of identifying people.

Here stands Gedalye Hempel. They cut up his eye, fractured his rib, and caused many wounds all over his body. He was hospitalized for several days, and to this day he has still not recovered and surely never will. One can tell from his face that not only his body, but also his soul has been thoroughly beaten. It is not actually necessary to lose a foot or a hand, to become a cripple, an invalid. From twenty blows to the sides and a couple of good strikes to the head and eyes, one loses something that can be more than a foot. This witness, nervous and uncertain, is similarly afraid to approach the defendants' bench and clearly identify the hooligans.

In private, they say openly that they know the hooligans, but they are afraid of retribution.

An elderly Jewish woman comes in, the mother of the accused Borenshteyn. Every forty-five- or fifty-year-old Jewish woman from Pshitik looks like she is sixty or sixty-five: a wrinkled, worn-out face, sunken eyes, and a terribly thin body. They are all grandmothers. She speaks quietly and calmly, but everyone is shaken. She paints a picture of how she went up to the attic with eight children and a six-year-old grandchild, how they all recited the *vidui* {final confession} in preparation for death, how her grandchild asked her to recite it with him. During her testimony, a scene plays out that repeats often in the courtroom. One of the judges, an avowed antisemite by the name of Plewako, asks the old woman Borenshteyn whether she has a son who is a Communist. She replies that she had a son who was a Communist, but he died in prison. She does not even let out a moan, but people can sense the bleeding of this mother's heart. An antisemitic lawyer jumps up and asks whether her accused son is also a Communist. The accused Borenshteyn jumps up and confirms that he has had a *shekel*[2] since 1917.

The Endek lawyers strive to prove that all Jews are Communists, and that the most terrifying Communists from Pshitik are those fourteen people sitting on the defendants' bench. It must be recognized that as soon as the word "Communism" is mentioned, it is as though the large-horned devil himself has strolled into the courtroom and cast everyone into a state of panic. Everyone somehow says this word in a special tone. The judges, prosecutor, and antisemitic lawyers all say it as though it were the most hideous crime in the world, as though it were the lowest possible degree of moral decline. This has a particular undertone: only Jews could undergo such moral decline as to become Communists. The Jewish defendants are terrified. They are not, in fact, Communists, but they sense that the smallest inkling, the slightest suspicion of Communism would be enough to ruin them. After all, this suspicion can blind even the most honest judge.

A Jewish man with a white beard walks in, barely standing on his own two feet. He had been in the hospital for weeks. He had pleaded for death to come. The angel of death was indeed standing by his bed, but departed at the last minute. He was not destined to be redeemed from life in exile. The hooligans beat him over the head with crowbars, not stopping until he lost consciousness and they believed him dead. Not until several hours later in a hospital bed did he recover, or rather, begin to feel his superhuman agony, from which only death can save him. What can this Leybush Toyber tell? He is still trembling and terrified, and they cannot get anything out of him. Nevertheless, this half-deaf old man was the living witness to who really started a pogrom, and who is capable of being wild, murderous, and bestial.

No matter how bestial, how murderous, and how cruel a person is capable of being, he is nevertheless still a person. Even these forty-four pogromists, who behave like bridegrooms, like heroes, like great fighters for the people; even these antisemitic lawyers, these genuine wild beasts, these truly wicked demons, who apparently obtained a university education for the sole purpose of making the beast within them quicker-witted, more sadistic, and cynical—they are all created in God's image and have within them a human spark.

---

2   {A certificate confirming payment of annual dues to the World Zionist Organization.}

It was sufficient to seat the witness Feyge Shukh before the judge. She is unable to stand, this mother who bore the blows of ten hooligans to prevent a club or stone from striking any of her seven children. This broken woman restored human form to these wild beasts. This Feyge Shukh, a woman of iron just half a year ago, repeatedly loses consciousness. How could you not, seeing your assailants strolling freely through the corridor? How could you stand it, when your assailants are called to testify that the other assailants, the ones sitting on the defendants' bench, are actually innocent little lambs who came to the market to look for a bride or for a relative's grave at the cemetery? She is thus unable to stand, and they allow her to sit before the court. That is enough. Does she need to say anything? Does she need to speak? Her entire broken, wounded body cries out that, in Pshitik, beasts went on a rampage, murdering out of a love for murder, out of bloodthirstiness, out of the thrill of beating the heads of weak people with stones. And yet she tells how she remained in the house to give all seven children time to hide in the attic. At first, they threw stones through the window. Then, they broke into the house and began beating her, a mother of seven children.

She was lying on the ground more dead than alive as the hooligans were about to leave, remarking cheerfully that Feyge was surely in the next world by now. Unfortunately, her body trembled, and the hooligans turned around and resumed the beating: "She's a strong one, damn it," one of them grumbled. If one is destined to live, one lives, and Feyge Shukh picked herself up and barely managed to crawl over to her Christian neighbour, a woman who had lived right across the street for decades. She begged her to let her stay for a while, but the neighbour drove her out. At this point, Feyge bursts into tears. Sure, hooligans are wild, that's natural, but for her long time neighbour Kasia to behave so bestially, that is too much to bear! She speaks, this shard. This remnant of a person has courage; she has a desire to speak and identify her assailants. And she identifies them: there are three of them, the leaders, the ones who beat her with crowbars.

The prosecutor proposes that they place the three men she identified among the remaining eight. During this operation, she loses consciousness. However, she recovers and again identifies the assailants. Inside this weak body, a vigilant soul is still alive; inside this battered, wounded head, a healthy brain is still working, and she recognizes everything, and she wants to speak and to identify. Yes, she is made of iron, just as the doctor told her as she was brought to the hospital in Radom.

It is not her body that is made of iron, but her soul, her spirit. The old Jewish spirit, forged from true Jewish belief, from Jewish faith and Jewish steadfastness. There is nothing new under the sun! There is nothing new in the world. Pshitik is not the first hell on earth, and the shattered Feyge from Pshitik is not the first Jewish victim. Worse things have already been seen: burnings at the stake, hangings, mass murders, hundreds of communities destroyed. Hundreds of thousands expelled and tortured. Feyge from Pshitik finds herself in very good company. She does not lose confidence. Feyge from Pshitik is sister to millions of brothers and sisters all over the world, and she does not feel lost during the Radom trial. It has all happened before, and much more is yet to come, and Feyge's faith will never be broken or extinguished.

It is hard to describe the orphan witnesses. It is even written in the Talmud that orphans cannot have mercy. It is only natural. I have seen Jewish orphans in orphanages, and pogrom orphans are not news to me. I have seen them in Kishinev, Bialystok, Odessa, Kiev, and many other cities. I have seen grown-up orphans and little children. But I have never seen such calm, reassured orphans as the children of the murdered Minkovskis. In the eyes of pogrom orphans, one could always see the clinging terror, the fear that seized and entrapped the child's soul. The orphans from the Pshitik pogrom give the impression that they do not yet know that dying means being lost forever, never again seeing their mother's eyes, never again hearing their father's voice. They are still waiting for a miracle, for their parents to return and bring them back to their own warm home. Their being true orphans could only be sensed in the courtroom. Perhaps they too only felt the true meaning of being orphans in the court. The murderers standing before their eyes must have conjured up images of their parents, and the axe, and the blood, and the screams, and the writhing and convulsing in a pool of blood, and the lying under the bed, and the watching and seeing them hacking into people with an axe, into a father, into a mother.

And so it was. The six-year-old orphan was thus unable to even raise his eyes to look at the murderers. The gentle words of the chairman and the requests of the Jewish lawyers are of no use. He is unable to look at the murderers, even to identify them. That is beyond what a six-year-old child can bear.

Meanwhile, the twelve-year-old orphan, Hershl, conducts himself truly heroically. He holds his big, dark eyes open, looking at all of them honestly and bravely: at the judges, lawyers, and accused. And he identifies the four murderers. He identifies them several times, in various poses and arrangements, mixed in with many others. He recognizes them so clearly and straightforwardly that even the evilest lawyers cannot twist their way out of his hands. He answers all of the questions concisely and clearly, not in a rehearsed manner, but from his heart, from his memory, from his sharp eye that probably captured for eternity both the wild faces of the murders and the horrifically bloodied faces of his parents. His testimony astounded everyone and will undoubtedly play a major role in rendering the verdict.

We cannot elaborate on all of the Jewish witnesses, but one thing was clear. Almost all of them came with marks on their bodies. Some were deafened or blinded by the blows, one had seventeen wounds and others even more, some had wounds in their souls and others had holes in their skulls. Almost all had been beaten, torn apart, ruined physically, mentally, and materially, with permanent traces that will last for generations.

1 July 1936

PART 2
OFFICIAL ANTISEMITISM

5. Government antisemitism

It is truly difficult to decide what to write about first: perhaps more on the Pshitik trial, where the Jewish name is defiled and mocked by hundreds of witnesses and about twenty lawyers burning with hatred; or about Minsk-Mazovyetsk, where the pogrom continues, in different forms, to different degrees, but energetically, with enthusiasm, joy, and laughter; or about the filthy, terrifying wave of agitation that flooded Poland more powerfully this past week, threatening far more brutal pogroms in the near future. Or maybe I should write about how the Prime Minister's legitimation on the dais in parliament of his nation's economic fight against Jews provoked a resounding echo among the ranks of the antisemites and reinforced their courage and energy.[1] Perhaps I should write about our horrible poverty and dejection, which are constantly growing, dragging ever greater portions of the Polish Jewish population into the abyss, progressively paralyzing Jewish life, and provoking increasing desperation.

I did not just make up this list of topics. These are all burning questions that torment one's mind and demand that one shout to the whole world, that one move heaven and earth, because together they signify that *the situation of the more than three million Polish Jews is becoming unbearable. It is becoming more than dangerous. The fate of the poorest but most vibrant portion of the Jewish nation is hanging by a thread and demands the attention of all the world's Jews!*

In our discussion of these topics, we will therefore keep at the front of our minds the weight and importance of these events and their significance for the condition of Polish Jews in the future. We will preferentially select small facts that convey major outcomes. Small events often shine a brighter light on the true situation than major ones.

---

1 {In the Polish parliament in June 1935, Prime Minister Skladkowski [Składkowski] said: "My government considers that nobody in Poland should be injured.... But an economic struggle? That's different." Quoted in Polonsky, *The Jews...*, p. 228.}

Here is a minor but characteristic matter. A couple of days ago, the official Polish telegraph agency distributed a memo to all newspapers stating that, following a Revisionist rally, street brawls broke out between Jewish Revisionists and Jewish Communists.[2] When a Christian procession passed by, the Jewish Communists tore the icon of the Holy Mother from a Christian woman and trampled it with their feet.

This was recounted by a correspondent from the official agency, an institution of the central authorities. The critical reader will recognize immediately that something is amiss: Jews are fighting among themselves, and then all of a sudden, the Communists toss the Revisionists aside and run over to the Christians to tear up their icons. Meanwhile, the latter say and do absolutely nothing. The next day, the official agency denied and retracted the memo. Nevertheless, all the Polish newspapers printed it; the antisemitic newspapers placed it under large headlines, with juicy interpretations and suitable appeals to the readers. Jews read it and waited for a pogrom to begin. In the current mood, given the Polish population's state of agitation, a single spark is enough to set off a fire. Given the Jews' state of agitation, the smallest incident is enough for them to expect a pogrom and see it before their eyes.

It goes without saying that no Polish newspaper printed the retraction of this fairy tale. Here is the part of the whole story that interests us: the official agency distributed an unverified memo that could lead to the greatest tragedies, that could ignite a fire throughout the entire country, that could trigger a pogrom wave that would make Pshitik, Grodno, and Minsk-Mazovyetsk look like trifles. We must acknowledge that, until now, it was not like this. The official agency used to be more careful.

Jews interpret this as a new direction for the government, a further downward slide on the part of official circles toward the antisemitic program of the Endeks. Jews have a dark interpretation, not because they are blind and see no light around them, but because it is indeed dark all around. It is pitch black and growing darker from one day to the next. The prime minister just recently tossed out the phrase, "economic struggle, by all means, but no physical mistreatment." It is worthwhile elaborating on the reverberations of this phrase across Poland.

---

2 {Revisionism was a militaristic Zionist movement founded by Vladimir (Ze'ev) Jabotinsky in 1925. It promoted Jewish sovereignty on both sides of the Jordan River.}

At the Pshitik trial, this phrase was cited not only by the antisemitic lawyers, but also by tens of Christian witnesses. A united front was created among the accused pogromists, the Christian witnesses, the antisemitic lawyers, and the judges on these grounds: *boycotting Jews is permissible*. It is not a crime at all. On the contrary, it is a patriotic act. The entire antisemitic press is dancing with joy: the government has permitted a struggle against Jews. The government even said "by all means," that is, it invited society to carry out an economic struggle against Jews. Well, it goes without saying that "economic struggle" is a very broad concept, and that the antisemites are highly skilled at reading into such a phrase many things, like beatings, stones to the head, and knives to the side. One antisemitic newspaper takes pride and boasts that it has achieved victory, since the prime minister is now saying what it has been preaching for more than forty years. It is certainly right that it has achieved victory. True, from a practical standpoint, nothing has changed. This whole time, the government has placed absolutely no restraints on the open preaching not only of economic struggle, not only of boycotts, but of eradicating and expelling Jews. The government itself ejected Jews from all official positions, from all the factories it monopolized, and from all the commercial enterprises it took over. Nonetheless, the newspaper is right to boast. Up until now, the government was still ashamed to admit that it was carrying out an antisemitic economic policy. If it is now no longer ashamed to call openly for economic struggle, then surely tomorrow it will not be ashamed to take on another few points from the Endek's program. Since we are living in fast-paced times, the development is happening very quickly. Nowadays, it is not necessary to wait forty years to descend into an openly antisemitic party. It can be done in forty days, sometimes faster.

The government is keeping quiet about the pogroms against Jews. Jews have no doubt that new winds are blowing in the "upper spheres," new winds that will further rattle the weak Jewish structure. They reach this conclusion first because under the new government attacks against Jews have grown more numerous and severe. Now, not a day passes without attacks against Jews in several locations, and the government keeps quiet, even though the current government is very talkative in general. Secondly, Jews see how the Endeks are feeling and acting after the latest pogrom in Minsk-Mazovyetsk. After the previous pogroms, they would at least take a break of several days from their provocations in the location where they had spilled Jewish blood, where they had punctured holes in Jewish skulls and Jewish houses. This time, they are acting entirely differently. They are developing massive efforts in pogrom-stricken Minsk-Mazovyetsk to reap with delight what they had sown with joy.

In addition to the legal appeal {for economic pogroms} that the Endeks freely distributed on the day of the first fair after the pogrom, there was also a secret illegal one that used entirely different wording. It called for an entirely different struggle, a physical one, and encouraged Poles to take advantage of Jews' flight by seizing the properties they left behind and preventing them from returning to their stores and workshops. On the same day, the Endek central organ, *Dziennik Narodowy*, printed the following:

> Minsk-Mazovyetsk must become the first major Polish city in which commerce and artisanry are transferred to Polish hands. The current situation in Minsk-Mazovyetsk is excellent and we must take full advantage of it.
>
> In a matter of months, we can achieve in Minsk-Mazovyetsk what will take years in other cities. The struggle must be carried out to completion. We are of the opinion that the administrative authorities will not stand in our way. After all, this is a matter of *economic struggle, which Prime Minister Skladkowski proclaimed legal in his government declaration.*

The newspaper concludes with enthusiasm: "We must immediately begin a major economic offensive in Minsk-Mazovyetsk. In the next weeks, if not days, new Christian stores and workshops must be established."

The newspaper further hints that houses, stores, and workshops can now be purchased from Jews at low prices. It calls on Poles to take advantage of the moment and seize positions. At the fair, the heroic victors walked around free as birds and agitated for people to buy from Poles, not Jews. They had no fear whatsoever of being disturbed by the police since, after all, the prime minister had given permission for economic struggle.

The boycott is even worse than a pogrom. It is no wonder that the Jews of Minsk-Mazovysetsk have only now become deeply worried and sad. Only now have they fallen into melancholy and despair. An ordinary Jewish man explained it to me: people were at the pogrom-fair; they saved their lives; they ran this way and that—a tumult, a din, with shattered windows, knocked-out teeth, dislocated arms and smashed doors. They forgot about their daily hardships—that life without a livelihood is worse than life without teeth, that without bread for one's children it is worse than without a head on one's shoulders. Gradually, the pogrom fumes dissipate, the holes in the houses are somehow stopped up, the pogrom "holiday" passes and the pogromless weekdays arrive, the ordinary days when one no longer receives a premade soup from the committee and no more bread is sent by wagon from the surrounding towns. Those difficult days, when one must *buy* bread, when one must *pay* for milk—days when one must earn and there is nowhere to do so; days when one realizes that tomorrow will be worse and the next day even more miserable—those ordinary, pogromless days are horrifying!

This man tells me he reckons that far more Jews are being suffocated by the boycott than were wounded in the pogrom. He elaborates a theory that dying of hunger is far worse than dying by hooligans' stones or knives. He lists for me Jews who stood in the market with merchandise, went hungry but lived, toiled away and coped with poverty. Now their stalls are shattered and they are afraid to return to the market. In a closed store, a Christian here or there will risk buying from a Jew. There are also, for the time being, few large textile or haberdashery stores owned by non-Jews, so people still have to resort to Jewish ones. In the market, however, in front of the entire antisemitic nation, when there are tens of Christian stalls with the same merchandise, what peasant would risk being a traitor to the nation? What Christian would have the audacity to buy a pack of matches or a length of thread from a Jew? Jewish market vendors and small-scale merchants of farm produce thus have no hope of once again eking out an impoverished living. They think with terror of the day when the aid committee will stop distributing bread and herring. What will happen to these hundreds of families who will never be revived in the Minsk-Mazovyetsk marketplace?

The official organs ensure that Jews do not feel protected or supported. For instance, a Jewish payment collector named Yekhiel Troyanovski worked for the municipal power station for many years. They fired him right after the pogrom. The reasons were unspoken but clear. They soon hired a Polish collector. A Jewish contractor worked for a military regiment stationed in Minsk-Mazovyetsk, completing various repairs in the barracks. Shortly after the pogrom, they drove him out. On 11 June—that is, ten days from the start of the pogrom and seven days from its end—they wounded several more Jews: Khaye Zusman, Yoysef Reyzman, Dovid Goldshteyn, and Meylekh Rotshteyn, a tailor. They split Rotshteyn's head open with a sword. The previous day, they beat the baker Radzinski, Avrom Herman, and Shmuel Zilbershteyn.

Hardly a day goes by without stones flying into one or two Jewish houses. In Minsk-Mazovyetsk, this is considered calm, and Jews can return to their hardships and livelihoods, to their plagues and dealings.

{Undated (1936?)}

6. The first ghetto benches in the universities

In tsarist Russia, the tsar and his ministers orchestrated anti-Jewish pogroms. Of course, there were antisemitic sentiments among the masses, and there was certainly no shortage of intellectual agitators and instigators. Nevertheless, pogroms had to be organized by representatives of the regime. The *passive*, unexpressed antisemitic sentiments among the masses were not enough to propel them to go out and beat, pillage, murder, and burn. The surrounding revolutionary atmosphere used to swallow and dissolve these kinds of passive antisemitic sentiments.[1]

In Hitler's Germany today, the ministers' most frenzied agitation and the open calls to pogroms by the highest-level representatives of the government are of no use. The population at large remains indifferent to the pogrom cries. When the government needs a pogrom, it must send its loyal servants from Hitler's party. Even when these servants drag Jews through the streets and smash windows of Jewish businesses, bystanders of all classes remain calm and indifferent and take no part in this "nationally" sanctified work.

We have an entirely different situation in today's Poland. The government fights against pogroms—weakly, tentatively, unenergetically, neither actively nor harshly enough. Nonetheless, nobody accuses it of organizing pogroms or aiding the pogromists. The pogrom wave is not imposed from above but rises from below, from the broad masses, the intelligentsia, small-scale proprietors, peasants, and the *déclassés*.

One can certainly level enough accusations against the governments of the ruling camp in Poland. The fact that they have treated Jews like

---

1   {See footnote 1, p. 15.}

stepchildren for years, excluding them from state enterprises and state and municipal positions, has inevitably created an impression among the masses that Jews are second-class citizens, or that they are not citizens at all. It is also criminal that for years they allowed the antisemitic press to agitate and incite and blame the Jews for all hardships and misfortunes. However, none of this changes the immensely important and dismal fact that the current pogrom waves have emerged from the broad masses, rising from below and endangering the current government alongside the Jews. One must not shut one's eyes to reality. There is truth in the words of a high-level official who said that if they wanted to arrest all higher education students who are active antisemites, they would have to imprison thousands of students, and if they wanted to arrest all non-student active antisemites, they would have to imprison tens of thousands of people.

The depth of the tragedy lies in the fact that the pogrom wave is expanding and spreading as a mass movement, like a powerful current driven not by agitators and provocateurs but by the masses. Of course the professional antisemitic provocateurs, who boast that they will soon be able to celebrate the fiftieth anniversary of their "national" work, are taking advantage of the antisemitic mood. Of course these provocateurs are, to a large extent, to blame for this mood of agitated antisemitism. However, it is also true that they have never had such easy successes as in recent years. The influx into the antisemitic parties has far exceeded the leaders' expectations.

It is also significant to note their activity and their readiness not just to speak, but to do. When one hooligan is arrested, ten more sprout up in his place; when one student is punished, tens more take his place. The more the government steps aside and gives in and keeps quiet and looks away and pretends not to notice, the bigger the pogrom wave swells, the bolder the antisemitic press grows, the bloodier the attacks become, the more numerous the victims, and the more discouraged and dejected the mood among Jews.

At the University of Lemberg, another Jewish victim has fallen: the Jewish student Iserduer was stabbed in the head with a knife. Her condition is critical. Several other Jewish students were beaten and wounded. As is known, the Lemberg Polytechnic instituted a ghetto for Jews more than two months ago: separate benches and separate rooms for laboratory work. The professors promised that this was just temporary. However, the new order was well received, and the student hooligans at the University of Lemberg undertook the adoption of this same reform. Attacks are taking place in nearly all faculties. They drag Jewish students off the benches. Those who resist are beaten and thrown out of the university. Other Jewish students do not sit at all, instead standing throughout the entirety of their lectures.

Fig. 7 Demonstration of Endek students at Lvov Polytechnic. The banner reads: "A Day without Jews: We will create an official ghetto." Wikimedia, public domain, https://commons.wikimedia.org/wiki/File:%C5%BB%C4%85damy_urz%C4%99dowego_getta_Ob%C3%B3z_Narodowo-Radykalny_Politechnika_Lwowska.jpg

At the veterinary institute in Grokhov {Horokhiv}, the situation is dire. The violence there is being led by two antisemitic heroes who had already stood trial last year for leading assaults against Jews. Attacks took place throughout the entire day in all courses. The student hooligans drove Jews out of the first rows of benches, threw their books and notebooks into the last rows, and did not allow a single Jew to occupy a seat in the front benches. All of the professors were "neutral."

In the trade school for hairdressers in Lodz, Christian students demanded that the teacher not call Jewish students up to the board. The teacher promised them that he would call up a Jewish student only after ten non-Jews. In another class in that same school, the teacher asked all of the Jewish students to leave the classroom because he wanted to consult with the Christian students. The school's director promised a Jewish delegation to put an end to these kinds of antisemitic acts.

Unrest erupted at the University of Krakow. The Polish students demanded that their Jewish colleagues sit on separate benches. The Jews refused, and the lectures were cancelled.

Fig. 8 First pages of the "List of Lectures and Exercises" for medical school student Marek Szapiro, University of Warsaw. The stamp above the photo reads, "SEATING in benches with an odd number." Wikimedia, public domain, https://commons.wikimedia.org/wiki/File:Index_of_Jewish_student_in_Poland_with_Ghetto_benche_seal_1934.PNG

Seven Jewish students were expelled from the Lemberg Polytechnic for signing the protest against the ghetto benches. The eighth, Altfeld, was not expelled because he had been brutally beaten. For that reason, he was forgiven the sin of protesting against the Polytechnic senate's unjust statute. They did not even listen to testimonies from the eight Jewish students facing trial; they simply read them their sentences. A large number of student hooligans waited at the Polytechnic, ready to beat their Jewish colleagues. Professor Kubitsky {Kubicki} hid the Jewish students in his office and summoned the police, who escorted them home.

A five-person band with one Jewish member had been playing in a well-known café on Novy Sviat {Nowy Świat} Street in Warsaw. Over the course of three weeks, Endek students created scenes there and demanded that the Jewish musician be fired. On this day, the café's owner published a letter in all of the antisemitic newspapers proclaiming his café *Judenrein*.

These are the hardships and terrors that are known. The list of unknown, unpublished suffering is undoubtedly longer and more horrifying.

18 April 1936

7. Ghetto benches

Warsaw's Jews have been on a break for two weeks. They are ready to celebrate the anniversary soon. For two weeks, people smashed heads and shattered windows, and now there is a pause. This is not to say that the beating has stopped entirely. They are still beating Jews, not in the main streets and by the light of day, but in the darkness of night. They are still beating Jews, but a few at a time, rather than masses at once, and three or four people are still being wounded every day. Nonetheless, three or four is not twenty or thirty. So, people are ready to praise God and those who helped the Almighty put a stop to a relentless mass pogrom. People go around asking how long this will last. To answer this question, one must know why the pogroms were halted all of a sudden.

Some say that those in high places gathered the leaders of the pogrom parties and advised them to stop, promising them a lovely gift in return: "ghetto benches" in the universities. The gift was accepted, and things soon calmed down.

There is another opinion as well: the Polish government was acting in the spirit of the program it has been following for the last two years. It permits people to beat Jews, break their bones, and destroy their property, but all in moderation. It does not allow the anti-Jewish pogrom to become a threat to state life as a whole. Two weeks in Warsaw, the nation's capital, a couple hundred wounded, another couple hundred mildly beaten, a panic seizing the entire Jewish population, disorienting and demoralizing Warsaw's Jews and dramatically strengthening the pro-emigration mood: the goal was reached, so they called it off.

There are people who believe that the protests abroad also helped a little. One thing is clear. Things calmed down as soon as the government wanted them to. Jews deduce from this that, if things were previously not calm, if people spent two full weeks wreaking havoc and beating Jews, then those who can so quickly and easily stop a pogrom had not wanted to do so.

For now, things are quiet in Warsaw. Jews ought to be satisfied. But no. An ungrateful people. They are not just dissatisfied. They curse the day when the pogrom stopped. The pogrom in the streets stopped, but on that same day, a different pogrom started, one that is far worse, far more dangerous, and far more painful. It led to horrifying results. The gift used to bribe the hooligans, the "ghetto benches," struck the Jewish population like a bolt of lightning.

It is difficult to comprehend, but it is a fact that despite the pogroms, which have been going on for more than two years already; despite all the restrictions in economic and political life and in the universities; despite all the declarations by powerful people that Jews are not and cannot be citizens with equal rights—Jews did not expect this officially-launched stone to their heads. They are dejected and humiliated, and they are just now beginning to understand the true meaning of the torments they have suffered thus far, as well as what this portends for the near future. One can read from Jews' backs their sense of condemnation and dejection. The Jewish back has grown even more hunched and crooked, and the head has crawled even deeper into the shoulders.

I reckon that all of those who criticized me for seeing things too bleakly, for painting pictures with too much black paint, will now criticize me for having shouted too softly, for not having foreseen just how far we could fall in Poland. I feel that it is my duty now to shout as loudly as possible that we are at the very beginning of the Polish Inquisition. After all, this used to be the demand of the opposition, and the government merely tolerated it. Now it has become the official program of the government.

Appetites are growing. Here is what an Endek newspaper prints:

> The directors' demand for ghetto benches was undoubtedly made with government assent. The Polish youth's resolute struggle was crowned with a resounding victory. The academic ghetto is a reality. The *numerus clausus* principle had already been realized. Sights are now set on a *numerus nullus*. Our entire front is moving forward! The

Jews are retreating all along this front! The first step in the fight for the de-Jewification of higher education is complete; the Jews will now sit separately. Full victory is not far off. We will be rid of the Jews.

The hooligans' newspaper is absolutely justified in its celebration. Their victory is indeed not far off. Last year, 10% of those admitted to institutions of higher education were Jews. This year, it is already down to 5 or 6%. The Warsaw University of Technology {*Politechnika Warszawska*} admitted 4 Jews out of 141 students in engineering, 4 Jews out of 97 students in electrical studies, 4 Jews out of 174 students in mechanics, and 1 Jew out of 68 students in architecture. The university admitted the following: 7 Jews out of 100 students in medicine; 11 Jews out of 350 in law; 13 Jews out of 105 students in dentistry. The situation is even worse outside the capital.

What are Jews doing aside from groaning and grinding their teeth out of their sense of powerlessness? The students decided to hold a seven-day strike. The Sejm and senate deputies went running to various ministers and returned with their heads hung even lower than before. One must recall that the current Minister of Education belongs to the left faction of Pilsudski's camp. The Jewish parties are also holding deliberations, but in complete secrecy, since every party is afraid that someone else will snap up this fight before them. Nobody has any thought of agreeing to a general struggle in this tragic and dangerous time. After all, how could proletarians and common paupers defend themselves together? How could socialists and Zionists sit at the same table?

This is still just the beginning. In about ten cities, the coachmen have also instituted a ghetto. The Jewish coachmen must stand separately, and in addition, the non-Jews wear tin badges on their hats proclaiming that they are Christian coachmen, that is to say, the bosses in this country, the ones with an illustrious lineage.

In still more cities, ghettoes have already been established in the markets. The Jews stand separately, and there is often also a sign proclaiming that this is where the Christians are standing, and honest, devout Poles buy only from Christians.

This year, they have also introduced separate benches for Jewish children in the public elementary schools. The patriotic tykes, eight-year-old and nine-year-old children, started dragging Jewish children to separate benches. In many schools, the teachers were absolutely delighted by the little antisemites and forced the Jewish children to sit separately. There were also teachers that calmed the little patriots down and told them to leave this matter to the grown-up hooligans. Such teachers were few in number, however.

The coachmen, merchants, and junior hooligans have decided for themselves that they cannot defile their "Aryan" (or foolish)[1] bodies by getting too close to Jews. It was the government, however, that decided that higher education students, the nation's future intelligentsia, cannot sit on the same benches as Jews. It is easy to imagine the upcoming proliferation of separate benches, markets, restaurants, theatres, museums, and God knows what else the hooligans of various types will come up with. Perhaps individuals will not even need to rack their brains to come up with ways of ejecting and expelling Jews. It is entirely plausible that the government will spare them the effort.

We find ourselves on the eve of immense and fundamental changes to the government and to domestic politics as a whole. Adam Koc, the "Führer," the creator of the Camp of National Unity, is preparing to become the true, and likely only, boss in Poland.[2] Consultations are taking place with Mr. Koc in the Presidential Palace all week long. From conversations with his lieutenants it has become clear that they are preparing to transfer power to Koc's group. The latter, which contains more than a few renegades from the antisemitic camp in its ranks, is preparing not only to adopt the hard-line antisemites' entire program but to install them in the seats of power. We can expect a real "salvation" for the Jews.

I must acknowledge that the leftist camp has not been sleeping either. It has been adopting pointed resolutions. It has been sending delegations to the Prime Minister, calling the workers to be on guard, and attempting to create a united front of all oppositional parties and groups. I would be happy to believe that this left wing is capable of holding back the black tide. To my great regret, I do not believe it. I cannot help myself. It is not that I am a hopeless pessimist. The reason is more profound: nobody believes it.

26 October 1937

---

1   {Leshchinsky puns here. The Yiddish word for "Aryan" (*arish*) rhymes with "foolish" (*narish*).}

2   {*Sanacja* politician Adam Koc announced the formation of the *Obóz Zjednoczenia Narodowego* (OZN; Camp of National Unity) in February 1937 and went on to become its leader. This nationalistic, antisemitic party subsequently won Poland's 1938 legislative election.}

PART 3
JEWISH RESPONSES

8. Jewish self-defence

What is the Jewish population's position on the attacks against Jews, on the hooligans that terrorize Jewish women and children? What is the position of the Jews on the government, which tolerates the hooliganism and allows wild young men to attack peaceful, innocent people with knives and clubs?

I must acknowledge that these issues were of greater interest to me than the attacks themselves, and even than the Jewish victims. There is ultimately much truth in the words, "in every generation, they rise up to destroy us."[1] Our response determines whether our enemies will succeed. A great deal depends on our response, our readiness to defend ourselves, to return blow for blow, knife for knife.

It is evident that different classes of the Jewish people respond differently. Everyone's response is, however, a national one, even if emphasis is placed on the class factor. They are beating Jews. Of course they go for poor Jews more frequently, since the latter veil their Jewish faces less and are more easily recognizable as Jews. However, the hooligans are certainly not operating from the standpoint of class. To them, every Jewish chest is good for a knife. For this reason, every call to respond to the hooligans with pride, dignity, courage, and strength is a national call that carries, and must carry, national feelings of unity and Jewish commonality.

We make this point in light of the fact that, naturally, the first to respond with brave words and calls for self-defence were the workers, who bear in their hearts the memories of the two Russian revolutions and are heirs to the revolutionary movement of 1905 and 1917.

One such group of Jewish socialists in Lodz spread a call to acquire weapons and organize self-defence. This appeal was of course

---

[1] {From *V'hi sh'amda*, a passage in the Passover Haggadah.}

disseminated secretly and illegally. We learn from this call that two people have died in Lodz, several are on their death beds, and there are many tens of wounded. One could not find out this much from the "legal" newspapers, which have now fallen into complete silence, having had their mouths sealed. According to reports, the hooligans there had a rough time. They were shown that beating Jews is, in any event, a risky enough business.

The response by Jewish workers in Bialystok was even more effective. There, the Nara members had to remove their uniforms. They were simply afraid to show themselves on Jewish streets in uniform, since Jews repaid them immediately for their attacks, or gave them advance payments. In the first days, the hooligans went on a completely unpunished rampage through the central streets of Jewish neighbourhoods. The Jewish population was not prepared. They did not believe that the police would tolerate this. At first, the Jews were somewhat disoriented. However, they quickly came to their senses and realized that the best defence is self-defence, that the best strategy is to rely on themselves, on their own power. They began retaliating as groups and individuals.

The regime soon realized that this situation carried a whiff of civil war and began arresting Jews, both the guilty and, far more often, the innocent. The guilty, too, are only guilty of protecting Jewish women, children, seniors, and weak people. They are guilty of having human blood and human dignity that drove them to respond to hooligans with the hooligans' own measures. Tens of Jews are indeed currently under arrest. However, in recent days, Jews have felt calmer, more secure and relaxed, since they finally feel that they are not only being beaten, but are beating too.

The pogroms in Warsaw were deeply tragic, with a large number of victims. Here, too, Jews became somewhat disoriented at first, fell into a panic, and relied on the authorities. After all, until recently, there was a very strong belief that, come what may, the Pilsudski government would not allow pogroms and acts of physical violence. As it happened, the ruffians beat Jews for a couple of weeks, their nerve growing ever stronger, and the holes in Jewish skulls growing ever more numerous.

The hooligans' nerve grew to the point that they seized a meeting hall in the centre of the Jewish neighbourhood, near Dzika and Muranow Streets. They even began storming into the neighbourhoods around the Iron Gate,[2] where the Jewish porters follow the sacred custom of defending the honour of the Jewish nation with gentile means, that is, with knives and clubs.

Then, all of a sudden, the patience of the Jewish porters, workers, and youth ran out. In general, from that day forward, one can no longer speak of a pogrom against Jews, but rather of a war between Polish nationalist hooligans and Jews. There were fights every evening for more than two weeks, particularly in the areas of the city where Jews live in compact masses. There were tens of people wounded on each side. The police claim that Jews beat the Nara members worse than the latter beat Jews. If only that were true. The assailed must, after all, occasionally lose their temper and exact revenge on the assailants. However, people closely associated with the circles in question assure us that it is not true. The police simply arrested Jews faster and in greater numbers, while treating gently the true hooligans, the instigators of the attacks, the agitators and progromists.

Here are several characteristic facts: on Stawki Street, the Nara members began to pick fights with Jews. Jewish workers did not wait for them to demonstrate their full strength, and instead gave them a good thrashing. Two hooligans were wounded. As a result, the police immediately arrested *several tens* of Jewish workers—every Jewish worker on the street.

There was also a fight in front of the Iron Gate, and people on both sides were wounded. Jews were the ones arrested, and four young Jewish men were sentenced to arrests of fourteen and thirty days. The hooligans started a trend of attacking women and children in the gardens in the centres of Jewish neighbourhoods. True, they often did not beat them; they had no need to. It was sufficient to start a panic that would cause Jewish women to run away, Jewish children to get injured as their strollers were overturned, and Jews in general to sprint after and fall over one another. The hooligans would beam with delight and mock Jewish women and old people.

Eventually, young Jewish men began putting an end to this hooliganism. And once again, the police arrested more Jews than non-Jews, although they knew perfectly well that Jews were not the ones

---

2 {The large iron gate demarcating the western border of the Saxon Garden; a prominent landmark in Warsaw at the time.}

who started it, and that Jewish men would never have done anything if it were not for the urgent need to defend themselves, women, and children.

Fortunately, there were enough conscious Polish socialist workers in Warsaw who understood that when the hooligans were beating Jews, they meant them too, and they joined the fight against the National Radicals. At this point, the fighting took on even bloodier and more brutal forms. The Nara members attacked the meeting hall of the PPS {Polish Socialist Party} and injured six workers. The PPS-affiliated workers paid them back, plus interest. The police arrested around fifty of the National Radicals. The fighting lasted for about eight days.

We cannot list here all cases in which Jewish workers and Jewish youth in general clearly demonstrated that if the hooligans are going to beat Jews, they had better be ready for a gift that will leave them in bed for a few days. So, what did the police do? They suddenly decided to conduct searches of many Jewish professional unions and arrested tens of workers. The following day, they announced in the newspapers that a large quantity of weapons had been found in the possession of the Jews, and that things would calm down now. They gave the impression that Jews were largely to blame. They summoned representatives of the Jewish newspapers and, as well as forbidding them to write about the attacks, they advised them to convince the Jewish population to remain calm, not to take revenge, and to rely exclusively on the police, who promised to put an end to the fighting. However, the attacks continue. The only difference is that people now know less, since the newspapers write nothing about them.

Here we are witnessing the responses to the attacks among the section of the Jewish nation that does not engage in official politics, but rather replies with its healthy feelings, directly and immediately. After all, it is only partially accurate to speak here about organized self-defence or about the direction of organized socialist forces. One must recall that, in Poland, there are up to 200,000 young Jewish men and women who belong to the Jewish youth movement. More than 100,000 of them attend a good sports school. This is an entirely new type of Jew who knows how to deliver a blow where necessary, and who refuses to let anyone spit in their porridge, much less their face.

So, how did the remainder of Polish Jews respond? The rabbis proceeded in the best and cleverest manner. They declared fasts. If the Jews do not eat, they will become so weak that there will be nobody to beat up. As Mendele Moykher Sforim[3] says, these days, the Jewish stomach is as big as an olive, and if Jews remain good and pious, they will reach the point where they have no stomachs at all.

This is certainly not only a wise answer to the question, but also a thorough one. As we can see, the rabbis kept their composure and immediately found a solution.

Far worse was the response among official Jewish politicians, who believed—or rather, forced themselves to believe—that the current government did not want nor need pogroms and would not allow them. These official politicians, who always covered up the government's economic antisemitism with its political friendliness toward Jews and its protection of Jews from the antisemitic groups that want to physically destroy them—these people truly lost their heads, feeling duped and swindled. It must be said that they had had a great deal of success among the Jewish bourgeoisie. Their theory had been well received; life is the main thing, and the government protects Jews and does not allow pogroms, so one must forgive its other sins. Alright, Jews will grow a little thinner. Things are miserable without a livelihood, but without a head things are even worse. Pogroms are the worst thing, and a government that protects Jews from pogroms is a good government. One ought to appreciate the government, defend it against its electoral enemies, avoid provoking it, and refrain from speaking out against it abroad. In short, one should be quieter than water and lower than grass out of thankfulness.

Then all of a sudden! The government is in full power, and yet people are beating Jews in the streets of Poland's largest cities; they are beating them openly for weeks at a time. They are publishing pogrom articles and distributing hundreds of thousands of copies. They are preparing brutal pogroms. And the government is silent! It refuses to even promise to put an end to it. It offers the reassurance that the waves of antisemitism in other countries are even worse. It was as if those Jewish politicians had been dealt a blow to the head.

The politicians who had themselves dismantled all Jewish

---

3 {Literary persona of Sholem Yankev Abramovitsh, the "grandfather" of modern Yiddish and Hebrew literature.}

organizations and representative bodies, who had cynically mocked the value of Jewish politics and Jewish struggle, who had ridiculed every Jewish demand—since Jews can only obtain by pleading, never by fighting—they are all now running around like poisoned mice. They shout that we must at least be organized and unified, but fail to say why we ought to organize or what a Jewish national council would accomplish if it were to emerge. They feel, however, that the masses must not be allowed to despair, that the chaos dominating Jewish life is a thousand times more dangerous than the hooligans' attacks.

There is absolutely no hope that anything will be created that would have authority in the eyes of Jews or non-Jews. Demoralization and neglect have profoundly corroded Jewish bourgeois society. Careerism dances the dance of the demons, not hesitating to perform hideous acts. Denunciation and licking of noblemen's boots have become daily occurrences in all organized Jewish communities. And there is not a single person in all of Poland whom people would respect and whose voice would be heard, not to mention obeyed.

{Undated}

9. Protests against pogroms

Anyone who has been reading the Polish antisemitic press over the last two weeks could easily observe a particularly joyful tone in the articles, a tone of victory, of success. Every day, they have announced that in this or that town, such and such a number of Christian shops and market stalls have opened, and such and such a number of Jewish shops and stalls have shut. Non-antisemitic, half-antisemitic, and even ostensibly anti-pogrom newspapers have also started publishing similar reports. The antisemitic papers have seized onto this, licking their lips and emphasizing that the entire Polish nation has begun to understand that the only way to help the poor peasantry is to seize commerce and the trades from the Jews. They make grand calculations that, if 250 Polish stalls and shops have opened in three towns, then 250 Polish families have a source of income, and thus at least one thousand Polish souls have a livelihood. They soon calculate that if they were to achieve the same results in three hundred towns, then 100,000 Polish souls would have the means to make a living, and so on.

Aside from this delight, one could also detect notes of an entirely different joy in their poisonous articles: the Jewish resistance has been broken. Jews are disheartened, lost, exhausted, and ready to surrender. This has added to the pleasure of the propagators of poison and preachers of hate.

Then all of a sudden—Jews are protesting! Jews are closing their businesses in protest! Jews young and old, radical and devout, left and right, all as one person, are declaring that they will not allow themselves to be slaughtered like sheep. They will take a stand, they will protect their women and children with their own bodies, they will use every means to defend all their jobs, sinking their teeth into every Jewish job and not capitulating to fear or despair. They will fight against every form of antisemitism, no matter if it comes from the highest levels, no matter if it is veiled, no matter if it is wrapped in the softest cotton padding!

It had seemed that the thicker the black cloud of antisemitism grew, the more dejected the Jews would become, and the more passive and discouraged Polish Jewry would grow. It was not only all the antisemitic parties, large and small, that counted on this, but also those movements and political orientations that claim not to be antisemitic and to be opposed to pogroms, but insist that we must reckon with the sad situation of the Polish peasantry, which is pushing and shoving its way into the city.

It has turned out that the persecutions and pogroms are not causing Jews to despair, but rather cementing and uniting all classes and groups; they are not humiliating the Jews, but rather strengthening their courage and stoking their desire to fight.

This would certainly be impossible if the Jewish masses did not feel that a great social and political game is being played out on their backs, that at stake is not only the fate of the Jewish masses, but also of the Polish working class and peasantry. Nowhere else has this game appeared as nakedly as in contemporary Poland. From one day to the next, the struggle grows clearer and more explicit. Either the landowners and Polish industrialists will succeed in deceiving the Polish workers and peasantry, convincing them that the main thing is the fight against Jews, in which case Polish Jewry is condemned to far greater suffering and tragedy than the German Jews; or, on the contrary, the revolutionary parties will conquer the minds and souls of the workers and peasants and bring about a leftist upheaval, in which case we will be physically, economically, and judicially saved.

This, however, is a topic that will need to be dealt with separately. Now we must describe how the last protest strike came about. This strike encompassed fully 99% of Polish Jewry and proved once more that all the miserable blows and insults that Polish Jews have endured in recent years have not broken their spirit nor crushed their ability to fight.

For three weeks, the attention of the entirety of Polish Jewry, all its classes and political movements, was concentrated on the Pshitik trial. It was, after all, not a simple trial about fights and attacks. On one side of the trial were the pogrom leaders and perpetrators, the educated pogrom agitators and the half-educated hooligans, brawlers, and assailants with knives—in other words, the whole antisemitic camp with its entire ideology and all its knife- and iron-wielding heroes. On the other side, for the first time in the Polish pogroms, the Polish population was brought to trial by a population consisting not only of people hiding in their attics and cellars, but also of true heroes with revolvers in their hands and iron bars wielded against the pogromists. For the first time, the elementary right of Jews to defend themselves, to respond to an attack by wielding a club, to meet a knife with a revolver, was on trial. After the pogrom cloud had been hanging over their heads for weeks and months, the fourteen Jewish accused sat on the bench for all three million Polish Jews and their elementary right to respond to an attack and to prepare themselves for self-defence.

Thus, Jews listened with pounding hearts to everything that was taking place. With gritted teeth, they read the open calls to pogroms by the antisemitic lawyers. With terror and fury, they read about the insolent behaviour of the pogromists and the open, shameless lies of the hundreds of witnesses. With joy and happiness, they read the proud speeches of the Jewish lawyers and, with even greater joy and indescribable delight, the morally elevated and politically clever speeches of the two Christian lawyers. They hoped and believed and awaited the moment when the sun would burst into light, when a Polish court would be illuminated with a humane verdict, with an honest, objective judgement. They wanted proof that in today's Polish Sodom, there are still virtuous men, true and honest judges for whom right and conscience stand above all else. Their nerves were wracked to the highest degree. The wounded Jewish heart was full of anticipation.

On Friday evening, before reciting the blessing over the candles, when most Polish Jews still experience an elevated, celebratory mood, and hope and faith find their way more easily into Jewish minds and hearts—in these pre-Sabbath hours, the thunder resounded. It is impossible to describe its impact. One phrase was heard from every Jew's mouth: *now for sure they're allowed to kill Jews*! In these words were fury, sorrow, endless anger, deep despair, and a huge question: how much further can they fall, this nation dazzled by the wild preachers of hate, misled by false providers and vile demagogues? Another question cried out from the eyes of every Jew: what threat does this pose to us, a verdict that frees explicit pogromists, that endorse knife-wielders and window-smashers, that leaves the Minkovski murder—a murder that screams to the heavens for a guilty verdict—unpunished, that punishes the one acting in self-defence ten and twenty times more harshly than the attacker?

On the outside, all Jews appeared dejected, downtrodden, beaten to the ground. But deep in their hearts simmered a feeling of protest, of struggle, of responding with honour, of demonstrating our power, our readiness to protect and defend ourselves.

This time, the right wing of *Po'ale Tsiyon*[1] correctly fulfilled the demands of the moment, and on their initiative, a general Jewish strike was called for Tuesday 30 June across the whole of Poland. The strike was declared for the hours from 12 to 2 p.m. and was {nearly} one hundred percent successful. A quarter of a million Jewish shops and market stalls and 200,000 Jewish workshops closed in unison across all of Poland. There were cases when customers had to be asked to leave the store. In many cities, this was a fair day, but the number of strike breakers and dissidents was negligible.

As always, the Jewish worker was the most active participant, the initiator, the awakener, the leader, but the entire Jewish bourgeoisie was willing to follow, as though unintentionally admitting that the future belongs to the worker, the sole class of Jews that has friends and partners in struggle among the surrounding population. In Lemberg, where there is such a relentless struggle among the bourgeoisies of three peoples—Poles, Jews, and Ukrainians—workers from all three nationalities demonstrated their solidarity for the hundredth time. In Bendin and Sosnovits, a large number of Polish workers went on strike. In Warsaw, the Polish workers from more than twenty factories went on strike. When Polish workers in a couple of factories refused to strike, a speech by a Polish or even a Jewish socialist explaining the political significance of this Jewish protest strike was enough to make everyone stop working. One Jewish factory owner told his workers that he would pay their wages for a whole day's work, but they refused and declared that they would make up the two hours of the strike.

One of the most important results of the two Jewish protest strikes on 17 March and 30 June was the fact that they managed to weave the struggle against antisemitism into the general struggle for freedom and a new order. It was demonstrated most unmistakably that the situation

---

1   {*Po'ale Tsiyon* split into left and right factions in 1920.}

of all of Polish Jewry depends on the victory of the Polish working class. At the same time, however, the exceptional situation of Jews was also made evident: the Jewish bourgeoisie, persecuted based on ethnicity and physically threatened, must appeal to and seek help among its social enemies—the Jewish and Polish workers.

Particularly noteworthy is the small town of Pshitik, which has suffered a great deal, but bears its burden with honour and dignity and increasingly displays its heroism. The entire Jewish population, including all women and children, gathered in the synagogue courtyard. It was as though the town had died. Everything was shut and bolted. Here they mentioned the fallen martyrs, and many people wept and fainted. But the proclamations of the speakers—*We are not broken! We will continue our struggle!*—provoked great enthusiasm. Among the speakers was Borenshteyn, who was freed not long ago. He was received with particular love and enthusiasm.

Joyful, encouraging news arrives from Vilna, Bialystok, Krakow, Novidvor, Mezritsh {Międzyrzec Podlaski), Prushkov {Pruszków}, Grodno—in short, from all of Poland—that the strike was a magnificent success, and that Polish workers everywhere demonstrated sympathy and joined the strike.

The protest strike was invaluable for Jews themselves. Their hearts grew lighter and their eyes brighter. It was a true pleasure to stroll through the Jewish streets and see the radiant Jewish youth, the invigorated Jewish working masses, and the joyful faces of ordinary Jews. I witnessed several scenes in which ordinary Jews, even well-dressed ones who likely belonged to the bourgeoisie, demanded that people who were running late hurry up and close their businesses. A special joy could be heard in that demand, the joy of a person who feels that he is not alone, that he can defend himself, and that he has allies in his self-defence.

Of course, the rubber batons of the police were not on strike. Wherever a police officer noticed that they were demanding the closure of shops or the cessation of work, he got cracking. Here in Warsaw, around twenty Jews were wounded and around twenty were arrested, and in Lodz around fifty were arrested. In general, however, the strike remained peaceful.

We commented that the entire Jewish bourgeoisie joined the protest strike. However, it must be added that *Agudes Yisroel*[2] called on Jews to fast instead and set a fast for the seventeenth of Tammuz, that is, a day when devout Jews fast anyway. The leaders of *Agudes Yisroel* thus made themselves look ridiculous, since their devout followers, who are sent to communities to supervise kosher food preparation, ritual slaughter, rabbis, weddings, and divorces, understand well that in the struggle for Jewish rights, it is better to follow the Jewish workers.

The Polish press, aside from the wildly antisemitic organs, has not yet responded. The antisemitic press is foaming with rage and threatening pogroms. A Warsaw newspaper (*Dziennik Narodowy*) writes: "This protest of the entirety of Polish Jewry against a verdict from the state court will certainly not discourage any Poles. On the contrary, we would like Jews to carry out protests like this 365 days a year, and not just two, but 24 hours a day." And after a poisonous description of Jews transforming convicted criminals into martyrs, the newspaper concludes: "The Jewish assault continues. But this will not discourage anyone." Another paper published a cry that Jews are organizing the revolutionary elements in the country and that Jews support the Communists and are fighting against Poland on the foreign and domestic fronts.

We must add that the verdict in Pshitik shocked not only Jews, but also Christians. Even the greatest Jewish pessimists had not expected such an absurd verdict, and even the most optimistic antisemites had not hoped that their allies would be given so much encouragement to perpetrate further pogroms. The newspapers tell us one fact that casts a glaring light on this verdict and shows us to what extent we can rely on protection by the central government. The chairman of the court, who throughout the trial conducted himself in a sufficiently objective manner and thereby gave hope of an objective judgement, travelled to Warsaw prior to rendering the verdict. It is believed that he delivered the "gift"' of the verdict under the direction of Warsaw.

22 July 1936

---

2 {The largest political movement of Orthodox Jews in interwar Eastern Europe.}

Poland is a strange country, so strange that I sometimes simply cease to understand what is happening around me. Consider the past week. Over the course of the week, Jews in Poland held as many as 400 meetings, conferences, and rallies, attended by no fewer than 200,000 Jews. They were evidently not afraid to attend meetings *en masse*, remain there for many hours, spend time together, debate, and often have a rather fun time, singing songs and dancing. At tens of these rallies, they sang the Internationale and the Bundist Oath,[3] that is to say, revolutionary songs. Nobody bothered them, nobody interfered, nobody arrested these singers who were, after all, calling for a social revolution.

In today's Poland, therefore, one is allowed to call for a social revolution, a free country! I can divulge another secret. At tens of the aforementioned rallies, people harshly criticized the government. They attacked the camp whose representatives sit in the government. They accused them not only of tolerating and permitting pogroms, not only of allowing the bourgeoisie to rob and exploit the workers, not only of letting the peasants die of hunger, so long as the privileges and estates of the landowners are protected, but of bringing Poland to ruin and delivering it into the hands of its greatest enemies, the Germans. They spoke, and nobody interrupted them. Freedom! Just like in a European country.

Here are a few scenes from recent days that ought to be surprising:

Large masses of Polish workers with flags and placards stretch across the streets of Warsaw. On the placards are proclamations against reactionary politics, fascism, antisemitism, exploitation, enslavement of the working class, and ethnic oppression. Alongside the Polish workers walk Jewish workers, a delegation from the Jewish trade unions. They too carry large placards in Polish and Yiddish. With these placards they protest against antisemitism and persecution. They demand equal rights for all ethnic groups. They walk through tens of streets, almost without a single incident. At one point, a couple of hooligans try to cause a disturbance, but they receive a generous portion of blows and slaps and quickly clear off.

Here is another interesting scene: a Bundist rally is taking place in a courtyard on Zamenhof Street. Three or four thousand Jewish workers protest against the attacks on Jews, calling for self-defence. They blame

---

3   {*Di shvue* (The Oath), the anthem of the Jewish Labour Bund.}

not just the capitalist order in general, but the current Polish leaders in particular for the pogroms. They call for a struggle in favour of a workers' and peasants' government, they sing the Internationale, and the atmosphere is one of revolutionary fervour. The representative of the Polish socialist trade unions, Comrade Zdanowski, greets the Jewish workers, calling for a common struggle against hooligans of all sorts, both hidden and overt, and promises the help of Polish workers in the Jewish workers' fight for full equality and the human right to security.

In the last week, joint assemblies of Jewish and Polish workers concerning the struggle against fascism, hooliganism, and pogroms took place in ten or twelve cities. A genuinely fraternal atmosphere dominated them, an atmosphere of struggle and revolution. I say this in all seriousness—an atmosphere of revolution. The members of the crowd were so ready to fight and sacrifice themselves, they were in such a state of elevated idealism, that one could almost believe that if they were called into the streets to fight they would go at once and struggle valiantly for their ideals.

The reader who has for more than two years been accustomed to reading about pogroms in Poland every day, and who is certainly aware that for weeks now a constant pogrom has been taking place in Warsaw, should not misinterpret my words as a joke. Likewise, he should not believe that the correspondents who have telegraphed or written about the pogroms are simply trying to cause him worry. But how is it possible that in a country where there is still so much freedom, people are permitted to beat hundreds of Jews and cripple innocent people without restraint?

I assure the reader that everything I have written above is absolutely true. There is still so much freedom in Poland. The trouble is that, in addition to the aforementioned freedom, there is another freedom. That is the freedom not only to speak, but also to *do*. Here is what that *doing* looks like:

From 10 to 20 September 1937, more than ninety Jews were wounded in Warsaw. We have names and news about their wounds. There are also tens or perhaps hundreds who suffered brutal blows but quietly washed off the blood at home and held their tongues. A wound remains in their hearts. A needle of shame remains stuck in their souls, pricking and tormenting them forever. This is because today's Jew is not the medieval

Jew who believed that the "goy" is a donkey that cannot be reckoned with like a human being.

Wounded? What does that mean? We will provide just a few facts, and the reader will understand immediately. At 20 Krochmalna Street, they beat Mendl Kaplan so badly that he remained lying on the street unconscious. They left Avrom Yakubovitsh (4 Pańska Street) with four severe, life-threatening knife wounds to his back and chest. Hersh Valkenbreyt had such a serious wound to his cheek that they needed to operate on him immediately in the hospital. In the best-case scenario, he will be left crippled. They threw the shopkeeper Kasher (20 Grzybowska Street), who was in the late months of pregnancy, to the ground and trampled her. In the Saxon Garden, they threw a young Jewish man into the water and he was barely rescued. Meanwhile, they beat a young Jewish woman, who lost consciousness. On Krolevska {Królewska} Street, Jewish higher education students Mark Kaplan and Pola Freyd were attacked. The assailants struck Kaplan over the head with an iron bar and trampled him as he lay bleeding. They used only their hands to beat Freyd, knocking her to the ground and kicking her until she bled.

The reader should note that this did not occur in some remote corner where a couple of hooligans encountered an individual Jew and beat him up. No. This is all happening on the liveliest streets of Warsaw. Groups of twenty and thirty hooligans walk along shouting, "Death to Jews! Go to Palestine! Get out of Poland!" They attack the shops, dragging people out and beating them, stabbing them, striking them with clubs, and destroying the shops' merchandise. This has already been going on for two weeks in Warsaw, right before the eyes of the authorities, and nothing is being done. This, too, is freedom! If freedom is for everyone, that is. The Polish rulers are consistent. It would not be fair to let the Jews call for a fight against the pogroms without allowing the others to carry out the pogroms.

It must be confirmed that in recent days a very appealing phenomenon has been noted. Jews are beginning to respond with iron bars of their own. They have recently wounded around ten hooligans in Warsaw. A few were severely wounded and will be able to tell their children that beating Jews comes at a heavy cost. This, however, is small comfort. We paid for every wounded hooligan with ten of our own. Even according to the most conservative calculations, Jews suffered material losses of several hundred thousand *zloty* in Warsaw over the last ten days. This represents direct losses due to destroyed merchandise, but the indirect losses are far greater. The Jewish bookstores have gone bankrupt because customers were prevented from entering. In general, in the pogrom atmosphere that has dominated Warsaw over the last two weeks, not a single Christian has set foot in a Jewish store.

Also in Warsaw, on practically the same days, there were street demonstrations by Polish and Jewish workers against pogroms and fascism, while tens of Jews were wounded and tens of Jewish businesses plundered. The government ministers themselves rode through the streets and saw with their own eyes that young Polish pupils were carrying out pogroms. They presumably also saw that Polish workers were demonstrating against pogroms, but they took neither of these observations to heart. Meanwhile, things have stayed the same. Of course, for every anti-pogrom demonstration, there are twenty or thirty pogroms. The Polish police cannot be blamed for this. They escort workers' demonstrations, ensuring that they are carried out as agreed and that, God forbid, nobody shouts anything impermissible. It is much easier for the police during a pogrom. They simply need to disappear, to become deaf to the cries of the assailants and the pleas and wails of their victims. It is no surprise that the pogroms are far more pleasant for them. It is enough to read the command of the Warsaw government commissioner, issued after two weeks of pillaging and beating, to confirm just how gently they speak to the hooligans.

Warsaw is not an only child. The same Polish government that allows Jews to carry out 400 meetings throughout the country in one week also allows what will soon be a full week of plundering, beating, smashing windows, terrorizing, and transforming Jewish life into hell in the town of Bielsk {Bielsk Podlaski}. After all, a government that does not stop a pogrom for five or six days is giving its silent approval.

A tragedy happened in Bielsk. A Jew, undoubtedly a scoundrel, shot a Polish worker. The whole dispute was over forty-five *groszy* {pennies}, and even if it is true that the Pole was drunk and about to strike him, the appropriate response is not to shoot him. On the other hand, tens of incidents like this happen in Poland every day, and nobody carries out pogroms against Christians when one Christian kills someone. In this case, however, a pogrom soon broke out and has now lasted almost a full week. The pogromists take a break and then continue their work. The police arrest a few of them and then take a break as well. Meanwhile, fresh pogrom forces arrive and carry on plundering and beating, and the police arrest another couple of them, but the pogromists sense that there is no real danger, so they head back onto the streets. Even though all the Jewish stores have already been plundered, they still manage to find a bit of hidden merchandise. If there is no merchandise, then Jewish pillows are also worth something.

Pogroms are highly contagious. Here is a scene that brilliantly encapsulates the mood among the population after two years of pogroms. In the villages around the town of Zloty Potok {Złoty Potok} in eastern Galicia, the Endeks spread a rumour that, for half of Wednesday, plundering would be permitted in the town. At dawn on Wednesday, hundreds of peasants rushed into town with sacks over their shoulders. The small number of police officers knew that they would be unable to cope with such a large mass of people, so they sent agents to tell the peasants that the plundering had been postponed until Friday. The peasants believed this and headed home peacefully. By Friday, enough police officers had been brought in and they let the peasants know that plundering would not be allowed. It must be acknowledged that the peasants were only prepared to plunder if the government permitted it. They had no desire to risk facing trial. If it's allowed, then by all means! If not, so be it. However, the most important thing here is that people could believe that a half day of plundering Jews would be permitted.

This is what the Christian population thinks of the government's attitude toward Jews. The Jewish population has their own unique perspective. A democratic Polish newspaper in Vilna writes that Jews are being beaten, but they have stopped informing the police about this, because it often occurs that the victims are transformed into perpetrators. The Jews are so despondent that they prefer to keep quiet. The newspaper provides the following factual account: on the corner of Pohulanka Street, two hooligans with clubs and brass knuckles attacked five Jews and beat them horribly. The lumber merchant Smolenski went to a doctor and it was confirmed that all his front teeth and his jaw had been injured. When asked why they had not stopped the hooligans, they candidly admitted that they were afraid they would face trial. Such scenarios have already happened. The hooligans claim that the Jews attacked them, and the police believe them and make the Jews stand trial. Then, on top of the lost teeth, one faces a couple months in prison. It is better to deal with just the lost teeth.

However, we are still at the beginning of the season. True, it has begun with a rather abundant harvest. September will yield an enormous harvest, but even now, a week before month's end, we can say that up to 500 people have been wounded this month. No fewer than fifty of these people will be left crippled. Five are likely not to live, and if they do, that is even worse for them.

In the winter, two groups will compete to beat Jews and force Jewish higher education students onto separate benches: the old hooligans from the Nara party, who spent all last winter tormenting Jewish students, and the youth organization of the Camp of National Unity, since nearly all ministers have by this point joined Adam Koc's party. The Camp of National Unity's youth organization is indeed led by a former Nara party leader, a proficient pogromist. The Koc youth have already made a start on their nationalist work.

They made their first attempt with Jewish windows. It turned out well. Two large display windows of Jewish businesses received a couple of large rocks. To prevent any mistake by the public, which was accustomed to the idea that only Nara members carried out genuine nationalist work like beating Jewish heads, windows, backs, and so on, the Koc group allowed themselves to be arrested and literally begged for their heroism to be announced in the newspapers. It goes without saying that these heroes were released on the same day.

They had even greater success with wresting the higher education student campaign from Nara, that is, dragging Jewish students from the right benches onto the left ones. In Warsaw, the Wawelberg technical school was founded by a Jewish convert to Christianity who also bequeathed funds for the school after his death. In this school built with Jewish money, the Koc group began their campaign against Jewish students. In order for the public to know who deserved credit for this patriotic work, they published a leaflet the following day in which they boasted that they had already succeeded in making Jews in one institute of higher education sit on separate benches.

The Jewish students refused this, but alas, what kind of a refusal is it? They remain standing the whole time. The Jewish students complained to the rector and he gave them a logical answer: last year, this was a demand by an opposition party, but now it is being carried out by youth from the same organization as the government ministers. How exactly could he speak out in opposition? How could he, a government official, speak out against the ministers' friends?

The chapter of "separate benches for Jewish students" got off to a rollicking start. In Lemberg, they would not let Jewish students into the office to enrol in the university. In Warsaw, armed fighters stood beside the university and greeted Jewish students with clubs. News has arrived from Vilna, too, that they are actively preparing for their winter campaign.

One must pay careful attention to the rector's words: now the club-work is being carried out by youth from the same party as the ministers.

We have presented our readers with two realities. In one reality, we have rallies, demonstrations, resolutions, fiery public statements, and revolutionary songs. In the second, we have pogroms against Jews, holes in Jewish skulls, knocked-out teeth, and fear of complaining to the police because one might end up in prison for a couple of months for "offending the Polish nation." We have ghetto benches enforced by an organization that belongs to the government's own camp. One reality is intellectual, the other, bloody. One is theoretical, the other, practical.

There is absolutely no doubt that the first reality, the humane, distinguished, liberating one, will win. The question is only how to endure until then. The first reality indeed demonstrates how much life-force, readiness to fight, and willingness to sacrifice Polish Jews carry within themselves. This might be their only consolation.

15 October 1937

10. Old-fashioned methods in new times

Times change among Jews as among Christians. Until recently, people believed that changing times were a good thing—we're moving forward! Every generation is smarter, more capable, richer in scholarship, and therefore better, finer, more decent and humane than the last! Well, there are few fools left who believe in these juvenile fairy tales of progress. It is possible to progress not for the better, but for the worse; to become not finer and more decent, but crueller and more barbaric. One can learn to fly not to be closer to God, but to drop heavy bombs.

We are aware of this because recent times have brought to light a long list of facts that, to those of us from the old generation, with old traditions and habits, appear so remarkably crazy, so strikingly bizarre, that we simply cannot make sense of them.

Take, for example, the old Jewish custom of decreeing fasts under extraordinary circumstances. If Jews were slaughtered or expelled from a country, if they were pelted with edicts and had nooses around their necks, they would fast and pray to God to still the hand of the slaughterers, to turn the heart of the wicked lord or king toward goodness.

There followed a generation of Jewish revolutionaries who ridiculed and scoffed at the fasters, penitents, and self-flagellators. One ought to torment not oneself, but one's tormentor! It is not one's own stomach that ought to shrivel up, but the stomachs of the assailants and instigators!

Well, what do we see now? Jewish higher education students who are beaten, bloodied, spat upon, cast out, and marked with yellow patches are fasting. Yes, they gather in their club, like our grandfathers in the prayer house, and they refuse to eat! They do not pray, but they do hold sermons! They do not weep or moan, but they swear that after the fast, they will turn to the fight. *After the fast*, after exhausting and weakening the enemy by leaving their own stomachs empty; after strengthening the fighters' hearts through their communal fast, they will go off to fight. They are satisfied with this, patting themselves on the back and calling it a "heroic fight."

I absolutely do not want to minimize the heroism of the Jewish students in Poland. However, I must admit that I cannot begin to understand what is going on around me. In our times, entirely different methods of struggle were applied to such circumstances.

Certainly, times change. In my day, non-Jewish students were leaders of the revolutionary movement. Now, they are leaders of the pogroms. Back then, non-Jewish students rushed to the barricades for liberty, equality, and fraternity. Now they rush with knives and clubs at Jewish students who have the audacity to mention these old-fashioned words. As an echo of the revolutionary struggle, the song of self-defence and death for the honour of the nation rang out in Jewish streets. Pogroms were, after all, the final gasp of a dying regime, tottering on its last legs. Today, however, pogroms are the cry of the young generation, of the future generation, of the majority of the intelligentsia, and therefore the majority of the nation's leadership. Perhaps the echo must ring out as hunger strikes and self-flagellation.

I am not trying to scold, and I truly do not wish to criticize. I am simply stating facts that ought to jolt us since they demonstrate that the world around us has changed so drastically that we have been thrown back a hundred years in the methods of our fight for the basic right to live, breathe, and sit and stand where we want.

It is tremendously difficult for me to write about this subject. I know that I am picking at an open wound. I know it is better not to think, to choke back all human feelings, to swallow all complaints about human honour and self-defence. I know one ought not to blame the weak for not being stronger. I know that mocking the weak is even worse than mocking the unfortunate. And heaven help me if a single cell in my body is bent on ridiculing or scoffing at someone. Yet I cannot choke back my lament that we have already returned to the ghetto, that we are once again people with yellow patches, princes of the soul who hunch down and convince themselves that they are still princes.

Who thinks about self-defence these days? Who thinks about human dignity? About national pride? Jewish students fast and Jewish workers' organizations—left-leaning ones whose members believe that they remain faithful to the most revolutionary traditions of 1905—merely clap their hands and celebrate the heroism and courageous struggle!

Am I really that old already? Am I really incapable of understanding these new times, this new generation? What is going on around us? Yes, yes, times are changing. New people, new songs.

Consider the following example. On the streets of Lodz, people are beating Jews. The hooligans doing the beating are ultimately a negligible minority. Lodz has 100,000 Christian and 30,000 Jewish workers. Jewish and Christian workers meet daily in factories, at strikes, during rallies, in city council, and in the unions. It will soon be fifty years of the blood and sweat of Jewish and non-Jewish workers in Lodz flowing so intermingled in the struggle and at work that it is impossible to separate the Jewish blood from the non-Jewish, the Jewish sweat from the non-Jewish. Tens of thousands of Christian workers are organized in socialist unions and vote for the Polish Socialist Party. Thousands of Jewish workers are organized in Jewish socialist parties. And in a city like this, Jews are being beaten! They have already killed more than ten Jews and wounded more than 200. Well, what is being done? The most revolutionary Jewish socialist party has sent a delegation to the authorities to *request* protection of the Jewish population. Yes, request!

I would go so far as to say *beg*. One can write, and perhaps genuinely convince oneself, that they demanded, that they insisted. However, I have reliable testimony that they requested: upon leaving the government representative's office, the delegation was intact and unharmed. This is the best proof. Nobody is going to convince me that representatives of *Agudes Yisroel* fall to their knees and kiss the rulers' coattails when they take part in a delegation, while the socialist delegation pounds on the table and threatens a revolution if no protection is granted. Of course there were *nuances* in the tone and the words, but since both delegations had the same result and Jews continue to be beaten, I am justified in saying that both delegations went to request or beg and had no success, which was entirely foreseeable. With regard to *Agudes Yisroel*, of course, there is nothing to be said. That is its very nature. But how can one comprehend a delegation from a revolutionary socialist party *requesting*?

I must repeat once again that I do not feel justified in criticizing or casting stones at people who doubtlessly hoped to accomplish something, to put an end to this nightmare, to make an effort. I understand well that one can lose one's head from powerlessness, from suffocating and choking on one's own strengths, from being compelled to squander golden revolutionary capital on trifles and petty squabbling in the ghetto. I know very well how despondent one can become, suffocating in the ghetto when one is fully ripe for the struggle, for freedom, for a decent new life, but must wait until the boss comes to his senses and gains sufficient courage and desire, for without him, one is nothing, sentenced to suffocate in the juices of one's own energy. I know that in such a fatally tragic situation, one can commit suicide and allow oneself to be led and misled by every mirage.

It is therefore not my intention to criticize the delegation's action, but I have the desire to shout: look what we've come to! Look how far we've fallen! Look how deep we've sunk into the muck!

Times change. And since we have before us an entirely new world, an uglier, wormier, wilder, crueller one, we too are changing, adopting different concepts and methods of struggle.

Here's another little fact that demonstrates how different, how much uglier and wormier the world has become, and how forcefully we have been compelled to adapt to this world.

There was recently a vote in the Lodz city council in which the Bund[1] voted with all of the other Jewish councillors. That is to say, with the whole of Jewry, with the unkosher, thousand-times-cursed and mocked Jewry as a whole. And the Polish Socialist Party voted with the National Democrats, with the hard-line reactionaries, with the bloodthirsty antisemites.

What exactly happened here? Did a bolt of lightning strike the meeting hall and split the councillors into nationally unified groups? There was indeed a lightning bolt. However, it came not from outside, but from the mouth of a representative of Left *Po'ale Tsiyon*. He introduced a motion for city hall to hire Jewish seasonal workers according to a percentage to which the Jewish unemployed are entitled. All of the Jewish councillors, including the bourgeois ones, voted "yea," with the Bundists joining the general Jewish faction. Meanwhile, the Polish Socialist Party unabashedly voted "nay," along with the National Democrats.

---

1 {Interwar Poland's largest diaspora-centred Jewish socialist party.}

After all, there is no need to be ashamed of such things in the year 1937! Even socialists are not ashamed to vote against the Jewish unemployed. Perhaps it is inevitable that Jewish students fast and Jewish leftist socialists request that the authorities protect Jewish lives.

Yes, times change! And how! You could just about lose your mind! And how urgently Jews adapt to the Christian trajectory, as though we have no life of our own, but only an echo of the life around us.

{Undated (1937)}

11. Suicides

It would be wrong to claim that poverty severe enough to drive people to suicide and abandonment of children in the streets exists only among Jews in Poland. One can read about suicides of unemployed Poles every day in the Warsaw and Lodz newspapers. Not long ago, an unemployed Pole in Lodz killed his two children with an axe and then committed suicide. Everyone cried that this man was driven to desperation by hunger, and after he had freed himself of his worries for his two children, he himself left today's ugly, repulsive world with a sense of relief.

Here is a description from a Polish newspaper of the situation in the Vilna region: "The number of children attending school is constantly declining. The teachers report that most children come to school hungry. If the children are not given food, the schools will have to be shut. Many of the children are dressed in rags. Typhus is already present in many areas."

Here is a description of how the schoolchildren in Polesia (Pinsk region) received food donations sent from Kelts region: "A portion of bread, five pieces of pork, a glass of cocoa. The little diners tore into it like hungry puppies. The teacher excused them, saying that hungry children cannot be expected to be polite." According to the report, a typhus epidemic has broken out in the Polesian marshes. People here are swelling due to hunger.

One could fill hundreds of pages with such facts, not only about the rural population, but also about the urban unemployed. There is a Hebrew saying that collective misfortune is a partial consolation. From a political standpoint, this can be interpreted as meaning that the hungry non-Jewish stomach will eventually extend its hand to the hungry Jewish stomach, and they will link arms in a united front, redeeming the world from hunger and servitude.

And yet, there is something about the Jewish suicides that makes them different. It can be very easily established that, among Jews, it is not those who are already hungry who commit suicide, but those who are frightened of the hunger to come. These people are weary not from prolonged hunger, but from struggling with the devil that is pushing them into the abyss, tearing the morsel from their mouths, psychologically tormenting them for so long that he exhausts all their emotional strength and turns them into playthings in the hands of dark thoughts and deceptive spectres. The Pole who commits suicide due to unemployment is *physically* depleted, while the Jewish boss who hangs himself in his *tallis* {prayer shawl} and *tefillin* {phylacteries} in a suite of several rooms is mentally exhausted. The former often commits suicide in a moment of despair, a moment of physical hunger. If he had found work that day, he would not have even thought about suicide and would have remained a healthy member of society. His soul is hardly disturbed or poisoned. The latter, the Jew, on the other hand, carries the thought of suicide around with him for months, often years. He lives in society for years as a sick, poisoned man, weary and despondent, and he poisons his entire environment, dispersing toxic bacilli and spreading existential dread and hopelessness.

This is the difference. The Christian suicide is a sign of poverty. The Jewish suicide is a sign of the sickness, fatigue, hopelessness, and mental depletion of an entire class of people, of a group. The suicide of an unemployed Pole is an individual phenomenon; the suicide of a Jewish boss who still has a maid in his home and whose daughters still wear furs, is a collective phenomenon, a sign of a disease that infects those around him. Of course, deep down in the soil, both phenomena emerge from a single root. However, remedies that are sufficient to prevent the despondent unemployed man from taking that step of desperation are nowhere near enough to save the Jewish boss from his step of resignation.

It is sufficient to give the unemployed Christian food for himself and his children, since he believes in the future and has not even begun to lose his faith in his class or his nation. The bourgeois Jew who hangs himself in his store because he has been twisting around for so long that the rope has ended up twisted around his neck has lost his faith in the future of his class. He does not need bread, and often still has plenty of it, but rather fresh courage, fresh conviction, and new living conditions that could give him faith in a future.

Here we provide several facts from recent weeks:

Thirty-nine-year-old Aba Shtern hanged himself in his brother-in-law's store. Who is this Jewish man? Was he left with nothing to eat? Two years ago, he was a landlord. His property did not give him enough to live on, since taxes were high and not everybody paid their rent. He sold the house and opened a store dealing in electric light bulbs. His capital wavered, and so did his hope to begin earning rather than consuming his small savings. The former landlord was no longer paying rent and he was in danger of being evicted from his home. Shtern put an end to the struggles that had exhausted his nerves. He leaves behind a wife and two children.

Shloyme Kalmen Hornshteyn was sixty-eight years old. He was a member of all of Warsaw's Jewish charitable associations, a long-time supporter of Zionism, a highly respected and active communal leader, the father of a large family, a major entrepreneur, a longstanding purveyor of produce for the Polish army, and a generous supporter of the poor and of cultural institutions. This sixty-eight-year-old Jewish man, with a long beard, was found hanging in his house, wrapped in his *tallis*. On the table, on an open *siddur* {prayer book}, they found a letter in which he asked them to forgive him for taking this step; he "could not bear it any longer." On Friday morning, Hornshteyn began his prayers and sent his wife to the store to buy something. She returned to find her husband hanging in his *tallis*. Was there not enough to eat in the home? They were not that poor yet. But it had already been several years since they stopped giving Jews army contracts. People go running to them, begging, offering lower prices, often even receiving a promise, but in the end a Jew never gets an order. That is precisely what happened here. After months of chasing and even promises, they finally told him on 28 March 1936 that he would not be receiving a contract. His nerves could not endure this. He lost all hope of earning from his old line of work. At sixty-eight years old, it was a bit too late to start a new one, and he had no capital. So he said his final confession, wrapped himself in his *tallis*, and left the world voluntarily. This distinguished and universally respected man lies by the cemetery fence; that is what Jewish law decrees for suicides. His family's tears and pleas were of no use.

Thirty-one-year-old Hela Dizenhoyz came to the house that had once belonged to her parents and in which she had grown up, and threw herself from the fourth floor.

At 7 o'clock in the morning, people in the courtyard at number 44 Muranov Street heard a cry of *"Shma yisroel!"*[1] followed immediately by the heavy thud of a fall. In a pool of blood on the ground, with a cracked skull, lay fifty-five-year-old Yoysef Goldshteyn. They found a note tucked into a buttonhole of his kaftan saying that he was being evicted from his apartment.

We could go on and on listing such facts, but it is absolutely superfluous. The ones provided make the picture sufficiently clear. The Jewish middle class has its back against the wall due to the crisis of the government's antisemitic policy and the surrounding population's boycott. It is severely agitated by the antisemitic provocation and the ever-increasing uncertainty. It has lost its faith in a better future and in its own strength. The Jewish middle class has lost its equilibrium and contributes a large percentage of Jewish suicides.

That is not to say, however, that we do not have normal suicides, people who are fleeing physical hunger and saving themselves from death by starvation. Here are several more facts.

The entire courtyard at 3 Dzielna Street was so horrified by the heartrending cries that everyone came running. They saw Avrom Khentshiner, a Jewish man, hanging in the air, holding onto the sill of a fourth-floor window. From all the windows, people began tossing pillows and featherbeds to the ground, so that if the dangling man were to fall, he would not be killed. The neighbours who had come running dragged the man through the window and into the apartment. Avrom Khentshiner has a wife and two children. He is all of thirty-six years old. He is a broker by trade. He hangs around in front of Jewish clothing stores and "grabs" customers. If a miracle happens and a customer allows him to lead them into a store and goes on to buy something, the broker receives several *groszy*. He knows, however, that such miracles are happening ever less frequently. He has no hope of a better livelihood, so he tried to throw himself from the fourth floor.

Perl Zilber, a mother of four children, committed suicide because it had been weeks since her husband, an apartment broker, had brought home a *grosz*. Her home was cold and there was nothing left to eat. On

---

1 {"Hear, O Israel" are the first words of Judaism's central prayer, proclaiming the existence of one God, the God of the Jews. The Bible commands that the *Shma* be recited during morning and evening services and, traditionally, a Jew recites the Shma immediately before dying.}

top of this, there was the threat of being thrown out into the street. So she decided to put an end to it.

Thirty-five-year-old Moyshe Shnitser, a bag maker, hanged himself, leaving behind a wife and two children. His household had long been without bread since the sole earner was unemployed.

Freyde Shustokove was a widow, a mother of two children, ages four and six. She did the children's laundry, got them changed, kissed all their limbs, then left home and committed suicide.

A police officer arrived on Smocza Street to evict the Kats family from their apartment. Upon seeing the officer, the woman, Ite, cried out, "What do you want? You're ruining us!" She then lost consciousness and died on the spot.

Losing consciousness and dying on the spot has become a daily occurrence among Jews in Poland. Not a day goes by without a dead Jew being lifted off of the street. Jewish hearts are not able to bear the hunger, the misery, the worry, the terror, and the desperation.

At 22 Nowolipki Street, fifty-six-year-old Yankev Oybentsvayg was found lying unconscious. He was taken to the Jewish hospital.

At the corner of Leszno and Rymarska, a thirty-year-old Jewish woman lost consciousness. It was confirmed that this was due to hunger.

In front of 31 Leszno Street, a sixteen-year-old Jewish girl was found unconscious. A doctor confirmed that she was exhausted due to hunger and cold.

Thirty-five-year-old Yisroel Zhema, from Ruzhany, was found lying unconscious on Nalevki Street. He was taken to the hospital.

In front of the main train station, a young Jewish man lost consciousness and died immediately. Based on a receipt from the tax office found in his pocket, it was established that his name was Henekh Mesing and that he came from Bzhezin {Brzheziny}.

An unknown Jewish man was picked up from the street, where he had lost consciousness. He died in the hospital. The doctors established hunger as the cause of death.

Sixty-three-year-old umbrella-maker Khaim Kenigshteyn lost consciousness by the door to his apartment and died immediately. He left behind a wife and three children.

Sixty-four-year-old Miryem Kaplan of 14 Twarda Street was standing and washing laundry. She suddenly collapsed and died. She left behind a husband and four children.

Twenty-six-year-old Sore Grinberg, an unemployed and homeless woman, lost consciousness in the middle of the street. A doctor established that she had collapsed due to hunger.

At the corner of Muranowska and Nalevki, ten-year-old Moyshe Goldman from Lekov {Łuków} was found lying unconscious.

We have provided here only the facts from Warsaw, and only for the past several days.

We have listed cases of fainting due to hunger. However, in recent times, a new type of heartbreak has also emerged. I have previously described the anguish and suffering of Jewish street merchants who are chased by police officers and persecuted by undercover agents. Just recently, such an incident occurred. A woman named Dine Kalber was standing with a basket of oranges. All of a sudden, someone shouted that a police officer was coming. The woman lost consciousness and had to be taken to the hospital.

Another few words about the epidemic of abandoning children—not infants, but two-year-olds, four-year-olds, six-year-olds, and eight-year-olds.

A boy of two years was found in front of the building at 4 Bonifraterska. In a note pinned to the child, his mother wrote in Yiddish and Polish that the child's father is dead and that his mother is starving and unable to look after him. She asked for merciful people to take pity on the child and raise him.

That same day, a Jewish child was found on Parisowski Square with a letter from the mother explaining that she had no choice but to abandon her child on the street since her apartment was cold and there was no food for the child.

At 29 Senatorska Street, a Jewish woman abandoned a child with a note in which she wrote, "I had to do this... Kind people, take pity and give the child food!"

Two boys were found in the gateway of 6 Niska Street, dressed in tatters and severely malnourished. They absolutely refused to say their names and where their parents lived. They were taken to the Jewish orphanage.

This is the appearance of the "Jewish street" in Poland, besieged by Polish antisemites and handed over as a bonus to the Polish masses so long as they drive out the Jews.

18 February 1936

12. Is emigration a solution?

I will never forget this picture: a tall man, around thirty years old or a little order, with a lean, weary face, walks along slowly, carrying a sign: "I am looking for work! It has been three years since I graduated from the legal faculty!"

I witnessed this scene today, 26 May 1936, on one of Warsaw's main streets. The man was, of course, a Pole. The passers-by shook their heads sympathetically, but nevertheless allowed the man with the sign to carry on walking. Everyone hurried their own way to fight for their piece of bread, to struggle for physical existence.

Here we have some news from Lodz: "The hunger strike of the sixteen men who barricaded themselves in the military volunteers' hall has been interrupted." What kind of a strike is this? And who are the strikers? Sixteen former military volunteers from the Polish army who had been unemployed for years entered the military volunteers' hall, declared a hunger strike, and indeed sat there for sixty hours without a drink of water or a bite of bread. The police eventually ejected them from the hall by force. Several of them fainted due to weakness. Will they get work now? We will have to wait and see.

These two examples are, unfortunately, not exceptions. They are eminently typical of the situation in Poland. They reflect most sharply the true situation in this country, the truly desperate situation of millions of people.

It is true, of course, that for every hungry Polish intellectual we can present ten Jewish ones, since the Poles still become judges, prosecutors, and clerks, and are also preferentially hired in state syndicates as well as private firms, while the young Jewish man who graduates law school must wait for private clients, and the competition is so great that he takes a mere half dollar for providing counsel. It is also true that the hungry Jewish lawyer would absolutely not have the audacity to go into the street with such an eye-catching sign, since it is certain that hooligans would beat him and the police would arrest him at once. It is true, too, that the percentage of hungry people among the Jewish masses is much greater in Palestine and in the Vilna region than among peasants in the countryside, where the situation is desperate. And it is true that the government thinks, *must* think, about those unfortunate peasants and will eventually have to quell their hunger. Meanwhile, it thinks about the hungry Jewish masses as well, but from an entirely different angle: how can we be rid of them as soon as possible? How can we force them to pack up their measly bags and clear out?

I agree, of course, that our hungry intellectuals and masses have absolutely the same moral and legal rights as Poles to be helped by Poland. I also believe with certainty that there will come a day when these hungry people will shake hands as brothers and put an end to this hell.

All of this, however, is only a political program, a propaganda program, a program of promises and hope. It is fine for those who believe that tomorrow or the day after, the socialist messiah will arrive and redeem everyone. But what if the messiah is a few decades late? Bitter reality has taught us well that he is capable of playing dirty tricks. Austria, Germany, and Italy are countries with large and powerful workers' movements. And yet the messiah refused to come, sending the devil in his place. And a devil does not readily cede the position he has captured. So if the messiah arrives late, if he does not hop on his donkey right away, what will happen then?

Then we must think seriously about an economic program for the hungry masses, about providing immediate help, help for tomorrow and the day after, and perhaps even for the day after that. If one takes this down-to-earth, concrete, realistic approach to the issues of Jewish life in Poland, rather than floating in the clouds or drowning out one's own logic and conscience with slogans and catchy calls to action, one reaches entirely different conclusions. If things are bitter for the surrounding population, they will be bitter and dark for us; if things are bitter and dark for the surrounding population, we will be buried six feet under, and perhaps even deeper.

From this standpoint, we must attend far more seriously and honestly to Polish voices that speak of emigration. It is not enough to shout the refrain that we are and feel ourselves to be equal citizens of Poland with equal rights, that all we demand of Polish non-antisemitic society is help in our fight for our rights, that we are not asking for advice about emigration and colonization, about Zionism and Territorialism. Of course, until they acknowledge the first part, our right to equal rights, they do not have a sufficiently clean moral conscience to speak about emigration. However, our task should entail not discrediting or mocking them, but rather uncovering the truth. Our truth consists of the fact that both fronts are equally important, that in the same years when Jews were fighting among the revolutionary ranks in Russia, they sent 150,000 Jews to America annually. There will be enough Jews for both a new, free Poland, and a new centre of immigration.

There is a conservative newspaper in Poland called *Czas*. It is far from an antisemitic paper. It combats hooliganism and regularly strives to say an impartial word regarding the Jewish question. Although we may have more than enough grievances against this almost non-antisemitic newspaper, we must nevertheless admit that it is a rare phenomenon on the Polish front. In the chorus of gnashing teeth, waving fists, and aggressive shouts that Jews are ruining Poland and the Polish nation, the tone of this conservative newspaper is more or less tolerable. From time to time, it is worthwhile to listen to this opponent.

This newspaper published three articles about the Jewish question. The point of departure was as follows: Without antisemitic agitation, without provocation, and without the pogrom atmosphere, the situation of the broad Jewish masses would still grow ever more catastrophic with each passing day. The newspaper paints a picture of the severity of rural poverty, the high rate of natural increase of the rural population, and the consequent intense drive of rural residents to move into small towns. The newspaper describes what we already see with our own eyes. The rural population is rushing with elemental force into retail in the villages and towns, as well as into artisanry and so-called *chałupnictwo* {cottage industry}, that is, work for businesses that is completed at home.

The newspaper believes that Jews are indeed stronger in terms of capital, experience, and knowledge, but the Polish population will nevertheless be victorious. This is especially so when it encounters "such fertile soil as the current antisemitic mood, the numerous examples from abroad, and political propaganda from several political directions."

While Jewish retailers and artisans are inundated by this rural wave consisting of poor peasants and the children of well-to-do peasants who have nothing to do in the village, Jewish mid-sized merchants and the Jewish liberal professions (doctors, lawyers, engineers, and so on) are in no less danger. Impoverished noblemen, children of fallen landowners, children of wealthy peasants who have received higher or mid-level education—all these people will surge into the Jewish domains of mid-sized commerce, medicine, law, and all the other higher urban professions.

Even if the government renounces the state policy it has followed until now and starts abolishing state factories and state commerce, it will bring little relief to the Jewish masses. That is because those dismissed from state enterprises will rush into private commerce, and into the private economy in general. These are, after all, people who have had excellent preparation, and they will therefore be even more formidable competitors. The aforementioned groups, which are at a higher cultural level and possess more capital, will also become strong competitors in large-scale commerce, industry, banking, and to an extreme degree in the liberal professions.

This picture that the newspaper paints for us is, alas, no vision of the future. It is the current sad reality. It only serves to confirm my opinion, which I have expressed in my articles in the *Forverts* more than once: antisemitism in Poland is not organized from the top down, but rather rises from the bottom up. It bears the character of a mass movement and it travels from the stomach to the head.

Czas concludes that the economic situation of the Jewish masses will inevitably become far worse, far more dangerous and catastrophic. "The Jewish population is in danger of starvation in the literal sense of the word," the newspaper concludes. The word "danger" ought to be deleted, since a very large percentage of the Jewish population in Poland is already starving, and the portion that is not starving senses that it is approaching that abyss of poverty with giant steps.

Where is the way out? The newspaper rejects all the hooligans' solutions and methods, all the remedies based on putting holes in skulls and banishing Jews. The newspaper sees emigration as the only remedy. It even understands that three million Jews cannot and will not emigrate, and it agrees that a portion of Jews will remain in Poland. At the same time, it does not say a single word about how the Jews who remain in Poland are to live or whether they will be treated like citizens with equal rights. In my opinion, it is of little interest to us what kind of future this Polish newspaper imagines for the Jews remaining in Poland. After all, we have no doubt that millions of Jews will remain in Poland and that we will have to fight for the masses to have full rights. The Jewish masses are sufficiently politically mature. Bitter experience is a good political teacher, especially when the Jewish masses have no trouble wrapping their heads around revolutionary ideas. That is not to say, of course, that we ought to shut the revolutionary prayer book and sit waiting until the Polish masses catch up to us. Political struggle cannot withstand any interruptions, waiting, or despair.

The danger is of an entirely different kind: we must not overestimate the value of the political struggle and entirely abandon the struggle for new jobs. And emigration must remain a prominent goal. We can see from experience that the millions of Jews who have emigrated from Eastern Europe in the last fifty years are living better lives than those who stayed put. I believe that American Jews, although they live in a bourgeois order, would nevertheless be unwilling to change places with the Jews of the Soviet Union. Jews have emigrated and continue to emigrate from Eastern Europe to more than sixty countries in all parts of the world. From everywhere—from America and Australia, from Asia and Africa, absolutely everywhere in the word—they send support to Eastern Europe. It is difficult to imagine the situation of the millions of Jews in Eastern Europe without the support of Jewish islands that have been planted in all corners of the world over the last fifty years.

We can learn from this that we Jews have no reason to fear emigration. Thus far, emigration has always played a positive and productive role in our lives. There is as much happiness to be found in the most distant lands as there is in Poland or Romania. The Jewish masses do not quibble; as many of them as possible set off for any possible destination. Over the last ten years, new Jewish colonies have emerged in the countries of South and Central America where there were previously only handfuls of Jews. These colonies are growing. People are already bringing over their relatives. Now German Jews, who have more capital, more technical education, and more courage to set off on lengthy journeys, have established new colonies in additional new countries. And one Jew sticks to others, so more people set off.

There is therefore no reason to be frightened when a Polish newspaper speaks of emigration. We must not respond by considering the word "emigration" non-kosher and declaring every conversation about it harmful.

After all, Poles frequently think about and discuss emigration possibilities for pure Poles too. They often repeat that it is a misfortune for Poland that the emigration of Polish peasants to America, Argentina, Germany, and France has been halted.

10 June 1936

13. Jews flee Poland

I do not want to be misunderstood or misinterpreted. I never wrote or said that Polish Jews *must* emigrate. That would be ludicrous and criminal. There is not a single party or responsible person in Poland who would say something so foolish and harmful. I am not counting the Revisionists and their leaders, who spout off phrases and shoot out empty slogans but are incapable of responsibility.

I did, however, say the following, and I will shout it a thousand times at the top of my lungs without growing tired: for Polish Jews, the emigration of 50,000 or 60,000 Jews a year is as necessary as air to breathe, as water in a desert, as bread to live on. This is a minimum, a number that holds out at least the possibility of staving off hunger.

It follows that 100,000 emigrants a year would be a great joy, a salvation. In ten years, even if no political changes transpired in Poland, this would radically improve the situation of the Jewish masses.

In the first case, emigration would remove the entire natural population increase plus an additional 10–20,000 people. We consider this a minimum because the entire generation currently coming of age has absolutely nothing to turn to. It is easy to say that we must stay strong, fight for equal rights in all domains, struggle for a new order in which everyone's needs will be met. But what are we to do with the 40–50,000 young Jewish men and women each year who turn twenty, twenty-one, twenty-two years old with absolutely no employment options? They want to live now, eat now, get married now, have clothes now. What are we to do with these tens of thousands who begin their life each year without a foundation, without support, without hope, without prospects? They are indeed taking part in the political struggle for rights. They are indeed contributing enough fighters for a new social order. However, one cannot live on political hopes alone. For that reason, thousands of Jews are rushing to all corners of the world, setting off on the most dangerous paths, literally risking their lives and searching. They find less than they hope to and even less than they need, but they find something.

Over the last fifteen years, up to 50,000 Polish, Romanian, and Lithuanian Jews have immigrated to entirely new, unknown countries like Chile, Paraguay, Uruguay, Venezuela, Colombia, and others. These were true pioneers who had no concept of these countries, their inhabitants, or their living conditions. They nevertheless set off for these distant and unfamiliar lands. And they do not regret it! Returnees are unheard of. To the contrary, one hears about emigrants bringing over their families and relatives, sending support back home, building a better and richer and more secure life in these far-flung new homes.

These pioneers who did not want to and could not wait for the messiah, for revolutions and upheavals, have achieved something for themselves and for all Polish Jews. After all, the political struggle of the Jewish masses here, which must be carried out, was not weakened one iota through the departure of these several tens of thousands of Jews. It was not even weakened by the departure in the last fifteen years of more than 200,000 Jews to Palestine and America. These 300–350,000 Jews who emigrated from Poland in the last fifteen years did not weaken political activity among the Jewish masses one bit. It is impossible to overestimate, however, how much they eased economic hardship in Poland. Their assistance for those who remain has saved tens of thousands of people from hunger.

Everyone is jealous of the emigrants. Everyone looks at them as though they are lucky, as though they are saved. Why is everyone jealous? Because the Zionists preach that they ought to immigrate to Palestine? Because the Zionists promise to build the Jews their own state? Because people like the writer of these lines believe that immigration is an undeniably important factor in Jewish life? No! There are far more important reasons, reasons that flog like iron whips, drive people to the end of the world, chase after them and force them to run, and drown out all clever propaganda and sage advice. Here they are:

In the village of Sandinyev (not far from Kelts), tens of thousands of peasants recently convened for a religious holiday. Jewish as well as non-Jewish merchants came and set up stalls, but before the Jews had even unpacked their merchandise, they heard shouts: "Poland for Poles!

Down with Jews!" The Jews immediately left the village.

The antisemitic newspaper that published this news was very pleased. Above all, it was pleased that the Jews did not resist and instead immediately ran away. They spared the Endeks the work of a pogrom. True, the Endeks are not lazy, and taking a knife to a Jew is a real delight for them, but for the leaders of this party, every pogrom is associated with unpleasantries. Thus, they are happy that they managed to achieve victory without a pogrom.

Politically speaking, this was certainly harmful. We must fight for every job, for the smallest rights, and, more than anything, for the right to live. After all, the right to do business is equivalent to the right to live. However, I would like to see the courageous Jewish revolutionary show up at this market, rather than sitting in the editorial office, writing that we must not surrender, we must not allow ourselves to be driven off, we must fight for the right to live. I would like to see this revolutionary, in the presence of thousands of agitated and provoked peasants, give a speech and demand that the escaping Jewish merchants unpack their merchandise and do business. For the time being, there are no such revolutionaries. We must remember: Why did these Jews clear out so quickly? Because they knew very well that Jews from Phsitik, Adzhival, Pshiskh {Przysucha}, and Adzhivilav and tens of other towns resisted, did not give in, did not allow themselves to be driven off, and they received blows and strikes from knives and clubs, to the point of pogroms—yet in the end they had to surrender.

In their hearts, they did not surrender. They remained deeply offended by the injustice, and as soon as they have an opportunity, they will take revenge against the true perpetrators of these pogroms and expulsions. But what did they do? What did they have to do from a practical standpoint? Should they have sat and waited until the Polish peasants and workers understood the true causes of all suffering? Should they have raised their hungry children with courage and the desire to fight hidden deep in their hearts? Should they themselves have been satisfied with the feeling of offense and the holy rage of revenge against the instigators and pogromists? Who will have the courage to propose *that* kind of pogrom?

Jews indeed carry in their hearts not only sorrow, but also rage. Not only resentment, but also the desire to fight. However, in the meantime, they wander in all directions in search of a livelihood, sustenance, employment for their children, and a secure place for themselves and their families. They do not run just to Lodz and Warsaw and the nearest large cities. They search for cracks through which they can push their way into Palestine, America, Brazil, Mexico, Paraguay, France, Belgium, Chile, Uruguay, Spain, Portugal, Egypt, and tens of other old and new, well-known and unknown, near and distant countries and lands.

There are millions of poor and desperately poor Polish peasants, workers, and people who have fallen in class status. If there were open gates to the United States, Canada, Argentina, France, or Belgium, they would have emigrated with joy and jubilation. There are millions of Ukrainians and Belarusians who are even poorer, unhappier, and hungrier. If the countries just listed, which are well-known and have already long been settled by large masses of people from these nations, were open, people would run there as though to paradise. However, the doors to these paradise countries are bolted and locked. So, they stay home; they do not try their luck in Venezuela and Colombia, Paraguay and Uruguay, Chile and Peru. Recently, 30–40,000 Poles have even returned each year from France and Belgium, pushing their way back into the hungry villages and languishing cities. These returnees with a bit of capital, with open eyes, with lively souls, with sharper elbows, are becoming the most dangerous competitors for Jewish retailers and artisans.

There are no Jewish returnees. Thousands of young Jewish men wander around Paris without a card giving them the right to work. They work under the table for half wages, scared of being caught and deported. They serve time in prison, as long as they do not have to return to Poland. When they no longer have any other choice and they must leave, they travel through tens of countries, begging and wracked with shame. They drag themselves from city to city, from country to country, and often from continent to continent, as long as they do not have to return to Poland. I know a case of a twenty-year-old Jewish man who travelled through eighteen countries and in the end still wound up getting hurled back into cursed Poland. Here, he was forced to try to sell neckties at the market, pulling at the coattails of every passer-by and selling a tie to one in a hundred, in fear of a different police officer every five minutes, having to hide himself in a nearby courtyard. I can assure you that this twenty-year-old migrant was far from the worst off. He was a qualified weaver, a conscious, developed boy, an entirely normal and healthy person, who could not extend his hand for a donation, but in order not to starve to death or throw himself into the river he learned—*had* to learn—to acquire support from the Jewish communities in more than a score of cities.

Why do poor Poles return to their poor, miserable home, while Jews run from this old home to all corners of the world, to unfamiliar climates, to the wildest places, as long as they can get away, as long as they can escape from hell?

Because in Minsk-Mazovietsk where, during a pogrom, they burned a Jewish stall and the Jewish community had to pay six *zloty* to clean up the embers, there is now a new stall, and the proprietor is the daughter of the local postal clerk—a Christian, of course.

What is the Jew who left Minsk-Mazovietsk, whose hopes for a livelihood in the city where he was born and raised were burned down along with that stall, supposed to do? Should he think about changing the political regime, or should he look for a livelihood in another city, or even in another country? Should he be ashamed that he is ceding a position and surrendering to pogromists, or should he exercise all of his Jewish strength, summon all of his inheritance of wandering, awaken all of his enormous capabilities and set out for unfamiliar worlds to seek a nest for his children? And should his teenage children sit there and wait until the Polish working class gains consciousness and the Polish peasants' minds open and they put an end to the pogroms and the Jews help them revolutionize the ugly, rotten world? Or should they follow the cry of their healthy human instincts and head to Palestine, to Birobidzhan, and even to the end of the earth, as long as they can build a new life, an independent life?

In reality, the three or four or five children of a ruined Jew like this, or a candidate for ruination, are distributed among several camps. The pathologically zealous, impatient one who has absorbed all of the desperate hatred toward the current rotten capitalistic order, who seethes and boils with hatred and impatience, turns to the Communists. To find footing on more solid terrain than the Jewish environment offers, he throws himself into the Belarusian or Ukrainian Communist Party. With fanatical obstinacy and truly insane fanaticism, he speaks only

Belarusian or Ukrainian in court and receives an extra couple of years in prison beyond the usual eight, and a couple of dozen bonus beatings on top of the usual ones.

He burns more with hatred for the old world than with love for the new one. The overturning of the old world is more important to him than the creation of the new one. Even Birobidzhan is appealing to him more out of spite for Zionism than for the positive aspect of its independent statehood.

His brother is also a fervent character, also with hatred toward the old order, but with immense scorn for Jewish trade, Jewish landlessness, Jewish status as intermediaries in economic and intellectual life, and Jewish in-betweenness and dependence even when it comes to starting a revolution. He has an enormous yearning for wholeness, selfhood, independence, creativity, security, and rootedness and is simultaneously laden with the full baggage of many generations' dreams and longing for redemption and the coming of the Messiah. This Jewish youth goes to the kibbutz, chops wood while singing, and lugs wooden beams with delight. Work and redemption become his gods, social and national salvation become the motors of his life, and he rushes to Palestine to build and create, and if necessary, also to die.

The third child is the calm, brainy, cooler-headed, conservative, sensible, realistic, dependent, earthbound, unimaginative, less self-sacrificing, gradualist, theory-bound one, the revolutionary inheritor of Jewish prudence and nationalism. This youth joins the Bund, which is so rich in foreign inheritance and so poor in our own, which wants to rebuild without revolutionizing, which wants to be brought to paradise rather than entering by force, which wants another world, a better one, but not an entirely new one, which out of all the Jewish cultural treasures from a thousand years recalls only one verse: "I do not wish to go free."[1] I do not want my own land. I do not want to leave exile.

Aside from these three, our ruined Jew from Minsk-Mazovietsk has another few children. A couple of them head to all corners of the world simply to seek a livelihood and sustenance. Who would cast a stone at them? Who would declare them traitors or cowards? And who would say that we have no need to care about them, no need to try to make their individual efforts of use to the community as a whole? Who would

---

1 {Exodus 21:5.}

claim that these ordinary Jews are stepchildren?

Living the hellish life of the Jewish masses here in Poland, one cannot say that we ought not to speak about emigration and that we ought only to explain to the Polish government that we live in Poland and will remain in Poland.

After all, what are the Jews of Pshitik supposed to do when, following the pogrom and the fine judgement in Radom, they received the "gift" of having their fair moved from Pshitik to a nearby village? As a result, several hundred Jewish families are left without sustenance, without hope of earnings, with no prospects of living in Pshitik. Should those few hundred Jewish families wait until the Polish messiah arrives and redeems them? Should they occupy themselves with political agitation, or seek the money to flee? And if we tell them a thousand times that fleeing is shameful and politically harmful, and, in any case, three million Jews cannot and will not leave, are they going to listen to us? Will they not look at us like crazy people, like people with their heads in the clouds who are unable to feel this hell on earth?

As I was finishing this article, I received news that a fresh pogrom had taken place yesterday, 2 July, in Dzhedzhgov {Dzierzgowo}, near Prashnits {Przasnysz}, with more than twenty wounded. It was during the fair and the Endek hooligans were exhorting people not to buy from Jews. The atmosphere was tense. Honest Christians advised the Jews to pack up their goods and leave while there was still time. However, the Jews were in no rush to leave, since they still had to live, still had to eat. If they did not earn, they would have no food. They held out until around 3 o'clock. Right when the Jews were starting to pack up, they attacked them with stones, clubs, and knives, beating and stabbing them. They seriously wounded a Jewish girl named Kirshenboym with a knife. Two Christians were also wounded, not by Jews, but because they were mistaken for Jews. The police force, which consisted of a total of three men, did nothing.

What should we say to the Jews of Prashnits who lived through a fair like this? That they should keep on going to the fairs anyway? And how could we stop them from thinking about emigration, from gathering the last of their strength and energy and trying to escape somewhere?

If the Jews of Prashnits, Pshitik, Minsk-Mazovietsk, Pshiskh, and Adzhival, along with many others, are thinking about emigration, then

Jewish society must also concern itself with emigration.

This does not mean, however, that all Polish Jews can and will emigrate. Millions of Jews must and will remain in Poland and they must therefore fight with all their might for full equality. Emigration is only a medicine to ease the patient's condition, to preserve his health for better times, and to refresh his strength, which is on the verge of depletion. One cannot live on medicine alone, but without it one might die.

25 July 1936

References

Aleksiun, Natalia, *Conscious History: Polish Jewish Historians before the Holocaust* (London: Littman Library of Jewish Civilization, 2021).

Anti-Defamation League, "Poland," 2023, https://global100.adl.org/country/poland/2023

Aronson, I. Michael, *Troubled Waters: The Origins of the 1881 Anti-Jewish Pogroms in Russia* (Pittsburgh PA: University of Pittsburgh Press, 1990).

Avrutin, Eugene M., and Elissa Bemporad, eds, *Pogroms: A Documentary History* (New York: Oxford University Press, 2021).

Avrutin, Eugene M., and Elissa Bemporad, "Pogroms: An Introduction," pp. 1–22, in Eugene M. Avrutin and Elissa Bemporad, eds, *Pogroms: A Documentary History* (New York: Oxford University Press, 2021).

Bacon, Gershon, "Cautious Use of the Term "Antisemitism"—For Lack of an Alternative: Interwar Poland as a Test Case," pp. 187–206, in Scott Ury and Guy Miron, eds, *Antisemitism and the Politics of History* (Waltham MA: Brandeis University Press, 2024 [2020]).

Cichopek-Gajraj, Anna, and Glenn Dynner, "Pogroms in Modern Poland, 1918–1946," pp. 193–99, in Eugene M. Avrutin and Elissa Bemporad, eds, *Pogroms: A Documentary History* (New York: Oxford University Press, 2021).

Leshchinsky, Yankev, *Erev khurbn: Fun yidishe lebn in poyln, 1935–37* [*On the Eve of Destruction: On Jewish Life in Poland, 1935–37*] (Buenos Aires: Tsentralfarband fun poylishe yidn in argentina, 1951).

Melzer, Emanuel, *No Way Out: The Politics of Polish Jewry, 1935–1939* (Cincinnati OH: Hebrew Union College Press, 1997).

Mendelsohn, Ezra, "Interwar Poland: Good for the Jews or Bad for the Jews?", pp. 130–39, in Chimen Abramsky, Maciej Jachimczyk, and Antony Polonsky, eds, *The Jews in Poland* (Oxford: Blackwell, 1986).

Penkalla, Adam, "The Przytyk Incidents of 9 March 1936 from Archival Documents," *Polin*, 5 (2008), 327–59.

Piłatowicz, Józef, "Anti-Semitic Resentments at the Universities in the Second Polish Republic on the Example of Lviv (1918–1939 AD)," *Cogent Arts and*

Humanities, 7:1 (2020), https://doi.org/10.1080/23311983.2020.1801369

Polonsky, Antony, *The Jews of Poland and Russia: A Short History* (Oxford: The Littman Library of Jewish Civilization, 2013).

Polonsky, Antony, "The Bund in Polish Political Life, 1935–1939," pp. 166–97, in Ezra Mendelsohn, ed., *Essential Papers on Jews and the Left* (New York: New York University Press, 1997).

Rabinowicz, H., "The Battle of the Ghetto Benches," *The Jewish Quarterly Review*, 55:2 (1964), 151–59.

Tomaszewski, Jerzy, "Some Methodological Problems of the Study of Jewish History in Poland between the Two World Wars," pp. 251–63, in Antony Polonsky, ed., *From Shtetl to Socialism: Studies from Polin* (Oxford: Littman Library of Jewish Civilization, 1993).

Veidlinger, Jeffrey, "Anti-Jewish Violence in the Russian Civil War," pp. 133–38, in Eugene M. Avrutin and Elissa Bemporad, eds, *Pogroms: A Documentary History* (New York: Oxford University Press, 2021).

Index

Abramovitsh, Sholem Yankev 131
Adzhival 2, 40, 46–50, 52, 57, 167, 171
Agudes Yisroel party 138, 149
Aleichem, Sholem 97
anarchy 21, 68, 98
Anczak 35–36
Anschluss 9
antisemitism 1, 5, 8–9, 15, 20–23, 25–26, 28–29, 32, 37–38, 43, 48, 52–53, 55, 57–58, 60, 67, 71–72, 83, 88, 94–96, 99–103, 110–111, 113, 115–119, 124, 131, 133–136, 138–139, 156, 161–162, 167
Argentina 164, 168
arson 58
Austria 9, 160

Belgium 168
Bendin 68, 136
Berlin 101
Bialystok 6, 16, 61, 93, 105, 128, 137
Bielsk 142
Birobidzhan 169–170
"Bloody Wednesday" 34
Bolshevism 16–17, 19
bombing 5, 20, 22–23, 45, 56–58, 147
Borenshteyns 50, 102–103, 137
bourgeoisie 16, 19–21, 85, 131–132, 136–137, 139, 150, 154, 163
Brazil 168
Brisk 2, 4, 37–39, 61
Bund 33, 150, 170
Bundist Oath 139

Camp of National Unity 124, 144
Canada 168

censorship 6, 23, 57
chałupnictwo 161
Chile 166, 168
Christians 15, 24, 28, 31–32, 37, 43, 45, 47, 50, 52, 55–56, 59–61, 64, 66, 68–69, 72–73, 79, 83, 86, 89–92, 94–96, 100, 104, 110–113, 117–118, 123, 133, 135, 138, 142–143, 147, 149, 151, 154, 169, 171
church 26, 40
Colombia 166, 168
Communism 19, 56, 80, 95, 102–103, 110, 138, 169
  Marxism 19, 34
Cossacks 16–17

Denikin 16, 18–19
deportation 168
Dobre 76–77, 87
Drohobitsh 62
Dubnov, Shimen 69
Dzhedzhgov 3, 171
Dzhevitze 52

Egypt 168
emigration 6, 9–10, 21, 41, 53–54, 57, 121, 160–166, 168, 171–172
Endek. *See Narodowa Demokracja* party

fasting 8, 131, 138, 147
Feldberg, Leyzer 90, 97–100
France 164, 168

Gast 63
gemora 25
Germany 9, 21, 70, 81, 115, 160, 164
ghetto benches 8, 118, 121–122, 145

Grinyevitsh 44–45
Grodno 2, 4, 24, 39–41, 43–46, 61, 110, 137
  trial 44
Grodno Society for Safeguarding the Health of the Jewish Population 45
Grokhov 37, 117

Haidamaks 16
Hitler, Adolf 29, 70, 81, 84, 115
hunger 16, 21, 40, 80, 113, 139, 148, 153–154, 156–160, 165–166

industrialization 8
  structural mobility 8–9
Internationale 139–140
Italy 160

Jewish protests 7, 36, 68, 118, 121, 133, 136, 139
  strikes 7, 78, 123, 133–134, 136–137, 159
Jewish Scientific Institute (YIVO) 69
Jewish self-defence 7–8, 39, 45, 52, 75, 81, 89–90, 93, 95, 97–98, 127–128, 130, 135–137, 139, 148

Kalisz 37
Kartshev 72, 87
Katovits 70
kehila 36, 43
Kelts 3, 30, 65, 153, 166
Khnidav 28
Klobutsk 76
Koc, Adam 62, 124, 144
Konske 52
Krakow 1, 61, 118, 137
Krasinski Garden 78
Kviv 30

League of Nations 10
Lemberg. *See* Lvov
Leshchinsky, Yankev 1, 4–8
Leshno 29
Lithuanian Jews 16, 166
Lodz 6, 34–36, 58, 61–65, 73, 77–79, 96, 117, 127–128, 137, 149–150, 153, 159, 168
Lomzhe 3
looting 2, 5, 84
Lublin 76
Lvov 7, 29, 117
Lvov Polytechnic 117

meshchantsvo 15
Mexico 168
Minkovskis 6–7, 51, 90–92, 135
Minsk-Mazovyetsk 2, 4, 24, 39–40, 46, 53–56, 59–60, 73, 83, 85–86, 109–110, 112–114
Mishlenitse 1–2, 59
Moscow 16

Nara. *See herein* Narodowa Demokracja party
Narodowa Demokracja party 1, 5, 9, 21–25, 33–35, 46–49, 52, 55, 57–58, 60, 63, 76–78, 103, 111–112, 117, 119, 122, 128–130, 144, 171
  boyovke 34
newspapers
  Czas 161–162
  Dziennik Narodowy 52, 55, 88, 112, 138
  Folkstsaytung 29–32, 59–60
  Forverts 162
  Haynt 28–29, 58, 60
  Moment 30, 60
  Robotnik 69
  Tygodnik Polityczny 52
Nove-Myasto 28, 77

Obóz Narodowo-Radykalny party 33, 35–37, 40
Opotshne 52
Otvotsk 67

Palestine 10, 60, 141, 160, 166, 168–170
Paraguay 166, 168
peasants 8, 16–18, 21–22, 26, 30, 46–48, 50–51, 78, 88, 90–92, 94,

98–99, 101, 115, 134, 139–140, 143, 160, 162, 164, 166–169
permanent pogroms 5–10, 56, 58, 61
Peru 168
Petliura 16–19, 40, 76
Pilsudski, Jozef 9, 96, 123, 128
Po'ale Tsiyon (Labour Zionist) party 24, 85, 136, 150
pogroms
  definition 2
  economic basis 15, 17, 20–21, 23, 43, 46, 49, 72, 76, 84, 88, 92, 111–113, 141
  trials 2, 6, 26–27, 29, 31, 36, 39–40, 43–46, 49, 52–53, 57–58, 63, 91, 93–94, 96–98, 100–101, 105, 109, 111, 117, 119, 134–135, 138, 143–144
pogroms in Russia 15–16, 20, 115
pogroms in Ukraine 5, 16, 20, 76
police 1, 8, 16–17, 20–21, 26, 34, 41–42, 46–48, 50, 59–62, 66, 69, 71, 73, 76, 79, 85–86, 90, 97, 112, 119, 128–130, 137, 142–145, 157–160, 168, 171
Polish Socialist party 7, 34, 69, 130, 149–150
Polish telegraph agency 35, 110
Portugal 168
Potvorub 30
poverty 80, 83, 109, 113, 153–154, 161–162
Prashnits 171
propaganda 46, 160–161, 166
Pshitik 2, 4, 6–7, 24, 30, 39–40, 46, 49–53, 72, 89–91, 93–94, 97, 99–105, 109–111, 134, 137–138, 171

Radom 30, 39, 49, 52–53, 63, 78, 91–92, 95–96, 99, 101, 105, 171
  trial 105
Radzimin 87
Rataye 25
riots 1–3, 72
Romania 163
Romanian Jews 166
Rosh Hashanah 75, 78

Russia 15, 20–21, 63, 65, 69, 76, 115, 161

Sanacja party 9, 22
Saxon Garden 4, 60, 66–67, 87, 141
Sejm 77, 87, 123
seventeenth of Tammuz 138
Sforim, Mendele Moykher.
  See Abramovitsh, Sholem Yankev
Shedlets 24, 63
Shenitse 73
Shvider 37
siddur 155
Simchat Torah 75–77
Skale 87
Skladkowski, Felicjan Slawoj 112
Sobolevski 26
Sosnovits 69, 136
Spain 168
stabbing 5, 29, 34, 37, 56, 62, 64–65, 77, 85, 87, 116, 141, 171
Stavi 30–31
suicide 150, 153–154, 156–157

tallis 154–155
tefillin 154
territorialism 161
the Red Army 18–19
Traugutt Park 66
Triskolask 76
Trzeciak 35
Tshenstokhov 3, 60, 62, 76
Tulishkov 28

Ukraine 16, 20, 76
United States of America 161, 163–164, 166, 168
University of Krakow 118
University of Lemberg 116–117
University of Warsaw 118
Uruguay 166, 168
Uyazd 63

Vala-Kurashava 26
Vaver 87
Venezuela 166, 168

Verniki 25
Vilna 3, 24, 32, 40, 45, 61, 69, 72, 79, 96, 137, 143, 145, 153, 160
  Duksht 24
  trial 45
  Vidzi 24
Vilna University 96
Vilnius. *See* Vilna
Vlokhi 87
Volomin 87
Volye 59
Votum Separatum 44–45
Vyelun 78
Vzhesub 30

Warsaw 3–4, 6, 8, 29–33, 35–39, 43, 50, 52–53, 57–63, 65–73, 75–79, 86–87, 96, 118–119, 121–123, 128, 130, 136–142, 144–145, 153, 155, 158–159, 168
Warsaw University of Technology 123

Yanov 29
YIVO. *See* Jewish Scientific Institute (YIVO)

Zamoshtsh 63
Zdanowski 140
Zhidlovyetz 29
Zionism 9, 24, 37, 94, 123, 155, 161, 166, 170
Zloty Potok 143

About the Team

Alessandra Tosi was the managing editor for this book.

This book was proofread by Annie Hine and Adèle Kreager. Annie indexed it.

Jeremy Bowman typeset the book in InDesign and created the EPUB. The main text font is Tex Gyre Pagella and the heading font is Californian FB.

Cameron Craig produced the paperback and hardback and the PDF and HTML editions. The conversion was performed with opensource software and other tools freely available on our GitHub page at https://github.com/OpenBookPublishers.

Jeevanjot Kaur Nagpal designed the cover of this book. The cover was produced in InDesign using Fontin and Calibri fonts.

This book was peer-reviewed by two referees. Experts in their field, these readers give their time freely to help ensure the academic rigour of our books. We are grateful for their generous and invaluable contributions.

This book need not end here...

Share

All our books — including the one you have just read — are free to access online so that students, researchers and members of the public who can't afford a printed edition will have access to the same ideas. This title will be accessed online by hundreds of readers each month across the globe: why not share the link so that someone you know is one of them?

This book and additional content is available at:
https://doi.org/10.11647/OBP.0342

Donate

Open Book Publishers is an award-winning, scholar-led, not-for-profit press making knowledge freely available one book at a time. We don't charge authors to publish with us: instead, our work is supported by our library members and by donations from people who believe that research shouldn't be locked behind paywalls.

Why not join them in freeing knowledge by supporting us:
https://www.openbookpublishers.com/support-us

Follow @OpenBookPublish

Read more at the Open Book Publishers **BLOG**

You may also be interested in:

The Last Years of Polish Jewry
Volume 1: At the Edge of the Abyss: Essays, 1927–33
Yankev Leshchinsky (author), Robert Brym & Eli Jany (translators), Robert Brym (editor)

https://doi.org/10.11647/OBP.0341

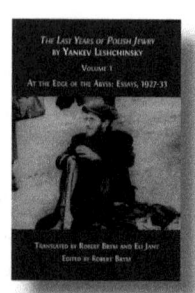

The Pogroms in Ukraine, 1918–19
Prelude to the Holocaust
Maurice Wolfthal (translator)

https://doi.org/10.11647/OBP.0176

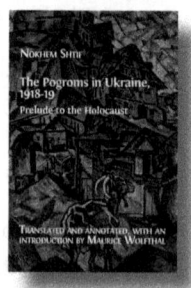

Photography in the Third Reich
Art, Physiognomy and Propaganda
Christopher Webster (editor)

https://doi.org/10.11647/OBP.0202

Brownshirt Princess
A Study of the 'Nazi Conscience'
Lionel Gossman

https://doi.org/10.11647/OBP.0003

www.ingramcontent.com/pod-product-compliance
Lightning Source LLC
Chambersburg PA
CBHW050243170426
43202CB00015B/2903